D1124824

HOPE FOR THE WORLD

CARDINAL RAYMOND LEO BURKE

Hope for the World

To Unite All Things in Christ

~

Conversations with
GUILLAUME D'ALANÇON

Translated by Michael J. Miller

IGNATIUS PRESS   SAN FRANCISCO

Original French edition:
Un Cardinal au Cœur de l'Eglise: Entretiens
© 2015 by Groupe Artège, Editions Artège
10, rue Mercœur 75011 Paris
9, espace Méditerranée, 66000 Perpignan, France

Cover photograph by
Piotr Spalek/Agence CIRIC

Cover design by Roxanne Mei Lum

© 2016 by Ignatius Press, San Francisco
ISBN 978-1-62164-116-2
Library of Congress Control Number 2016934631
Printed in the United States of America ∞

Acknowledgments

Cardinal Raymond Leo Burke thanks
Father Michael Joseph Houser and Abbé Ryan Post
for their important assistance.

Guillaume d'Alançon thanks Father Marc
for his expertise in English.

Contents

Introduction

As soon as you enter the apartment of Cardinal Raymond Leo Burke, your glance is drawn to a good-sized picture of Pope Francis.

The Cardinal has spent his whole life serving the Church and the popes. In 1975, Paul VI ordained him a priest in Saint Peter's Basilica in Rome, and twenty years later, in the same place, John Paul II consecrated him a bishop for the Diocese of La Crosse, Wisconsin, in the United States. That was on January 6, 1995. Just a minor detail: the new bishop was installed on February 22 of that year, on the Feast of the Chair of Saint Peter.

Not many cardinals today received priestly ordination and episcopal consecration from two Supreme Pontiffs who are now elevated to the honor of the altars. It is difficult to imagine that this has not created a special bond with the Vicar of Christ and everything for which he stands. And there is more. On December 2, 2003, Bishop Raymond Leo Burke was appointed Archbishop of Saint Louis, Missouri; on June 29, 2004, he received the pallium from the hands of John Paul II. On May 6, 2008, Benedict XVI appointed him, in addition to his duties as an Ordinary, to serve as a member of the Congregation for the Clergy and the Pontifical Council for Legislative Texts. On June 27 of the same year, the

9

Pope appointed him Prefect of the Supreme Tribunal of the Apostolic Signatura. During the Consistory of November 20, 2010, he was created a cardinal.

Providence speaks through facts, through the present reality, through what is said and done, through what is experienced. For forty years, Raymond Leo Burke has been working humbly in the Lord's vineyard. Those who have been close to him know that he is a gentle, compassionate pastor who intends to spare no effort for Christ and His Church for the sake of the salvation of souls. In bioethical terms, this is the reason why he says that the defense of truth is inseparable from the active protection of human life from conception until its natural end. To want to proclaim the Gospel is to want to live the Gospel; there is no dialectic between doctrine and pastoral care. This is where real poverty, true simplicity is found. When Christ invites the rich young man to give up his material advantages to follow Him, His word is pastoral and doctrinal at the same time. Where a mere canonist might observe a gap in the law, the theologian and pastor discovers a mystery to be studied in greater depth. God's silence is what invites the human person to take up his cross to follow Him. Many who have worked closely with Cardinal Burke testify that he does not have the faults of an intransigent judge: this is a profoundly spiritual man and a good listener. His deep devotion to the Sacred Heart of Jesus and the Immaculate Heart of Mary give a very special weight to his conversations. Often, as an ejaculatory prayer, one hears him repeat all the love that he has for Christ, Who is meek and humble of heart. That is true theology, learned in the school of Saint John, the beloved disciple who loved to lean on the Sacred Heart so as to hear its secrets. All the saints are theologians, only the saints are theologians . . . In a homily that he gave in 2013 in Saint Cecilia Abbey in Solesmes, France, the Cardinal summarized the essential thing in one sentence:

> Jesus, the Son, is the door situated between the Father and Christian souls. There is no other. Jesus is the door through which the praises and sacrifices of souls ascend to the Father and through which choice graces, the fruits of the infinite merits of the God-man, descend upon the world.

He continued:

> Let us turn our attention to the lock of this door, namely, the Sacred Heart. In order to open the door, we must strive to know the secrets of this divine Heart, which has loved men so much.

During the Extraordinary Synod of Bishops on the Family that took place from October 5 to 19, 2014, the Cardinal was appointed a Synod Father by the Supreme Pontiff. Between the plenary sessions, the bishops met in smaller groups according to language. He was then chosen as moderator of an English-speaking working group. As *Cardinal Patronus* of the Sovereign Military Order of Malta since November 8, 2014, he carries out his mission as a gift from Providence, as he himself confided to us. A fervent defender of the family and of human life—we remember his magisterial speech given in Biarritz, France, in 2012—he would accept his new responsibility, certain that service to the weakest is an act of adoring God. Like the sun that never sets on the Order of Malta, which is present in the four corners of the world, divine mercy is for all who seek to model their lives on that of Jesus Christ. This appointment may have been surprising. What is striking is the way in which the person most affected by the appointment understands it. For an outsider, the news was astonishing. The Cardinal admitted to me that, the morning after the day when he had received from the Pope the announcement of this appointment, he was greatly at peace. He had immediately entrusted himself to the Lord, and, ever since that moment, he has experienced this change on the supernatural level. What a wonderful lesson for the rest of us, I said to myself. Whereas a concern about making an attractive impression so as to advance one's career deeply damages authentic missionary zeal, the Cardinal's response was that of an interior man whose life is not his own. *Fiat voluntas tua*. Thy will be done.

There is another very recent sign that is unmistakable. Pope Emeritus Benedict XVI addressed a message to those who organized the *Summorum Pontificum* pilgrimage to Rome. This message was read on the occasion of the Mass on October 25, 2014, celebrated by His Eminence Cardinal Raymond Leo Burke at the altar of the Chair of Saint Peter in the Basilica by the same name. Here is the text of it:

> I am very happy that the *usus antiquus* is alive today in complete peace with the Church, even among young people, supported and celebrated by great cardinals. Spiritually I will be with you. My status as a "cloistered monk" does not allow me to be present outside. I leave my cloister only on special occasions, when invited personally by the Pope.

A "great cardinal" who, in talking about questions concerning the family and human life, only restates what Saint John Paul II would have said if he had been invited to the Extraordinary Synod as one bishop among the others. And we know how forcefully the Archbishop of Kraków could speak to his detractors. Once he became Pope, he did not change his tone when it was a matter of defending the faith and morality and, thus, ran the risk of cutting himself off "emotionally" from many bishops who were probably afflicted with some of the maladies described by Pope Francis on December 22, 2014, during the presentation of his Christmas greetings to the Curia. For, although human beings change, the family does not change and God's plan remains. While participating in a group reflection on the questionnaire sent to the dioceses of the world, one mother of a family, disappointed by the drift of the discussion, exclaimed: "But when all is said and done, who has the words of everlasting life? Man or God?" She continued: "Maybe we should ask ourselves, too, whether we are listening to what God wants to tell us, instead of just trying to assert our paltry claims!" I think she got that right. In an interview in March 2015, another "great cardinal", currently the Prefect of the Congregation for Divine Worship, Robert Sarah, invited Christians to rely on Christ, whatever the circumstances may be in which the Church is tossed about:

> It is necessary to be serene and calm, for in the boat that he [the Pope] is steering, there is Jesus with him, who said to Peter: "I have prayed for you that your faith may not fail; and when you have turned again, strengthen your brethren."

In order to be proclaimed, this faith needs the Sacred Liturgy. Faithful to the great tradition of the Church, Cardinal Burke has adopted the liturgical advances made by Benedict XVI, just as Pope Francis has done. Responding to a question from a journalist, the same Cardinal Sarah echoed the Supreme Pontiff:

> Pope Francis told me that Benedict XVI had started an excellent work along this liturgical line and that it was necessary to continue it.

Does the shepherd not perform a liturgical work when he gathers his flock and leads it to the sunny pastures on the high plateaus? As they are about to set out, he sits in front of his cabin and inspects the hooves of his sheep and takes care of them if necessary; a mystery of mercy. Then, accompanied by his dogs, like so many guardian angels, he leaves the shady valley to go to the heights. The climb is challenging, like suffering. This is the sacrifice of the shepherd who does his work well and says together with the Good Shepherd: "I have guarded them, and none of them is lost" (Jn 17:12).

Cardinal Burke is indeed familiar with the pastoral allegory, since he spent his childhood in the midst of cows. Prolonged contact with creation made him a friend of beauty: he loves to celebrate Holy Mass with a peaceful *ars celebrandi*, preferring harmony, as the saintly Curé of Ars did, to the undignified pauperism that is closer to the art prescribed by Stalin and Ceaușescu than to Cistercian sobriety.

At the end of my last meeting with the Cardinal, descending the stairs of his apartment, which is a short distance from Saint Peter's Square, the most beautiful church in the world,

I was giving thanks. The setting sun crowned the dome of the Basilica.

— Guillaume d'Alançon
August 15, 2015
Solemnity of the Assumption
of the Blessed Virgin Mary

PART ONE

The Lord's Call

To begin this interview, Your Eminence, could you tell us in a few words the story of your vocation? How did your parents and family play a role in your becoming aware of the Lord's call? And from what region do you come?

I am an American, son of a farmer, of Irish descent. My paternal grandmother left her home in Cullen, in County Cork, Ireland, in the late 1880s. My paternal great-grandfather had left his home in Ballygriffin, in County Tipperary, Ireland, in the early nineteenth century.

My mother's family had emigrated from England long before that, and they were Protestants. My mother had been raised in the American Baptist Church. Her mother, the only one of all my grandparents with whom I had a chance to be acquainted, although she died when I was seven years old, was a pious Christian, to whom my mother was very close. When my mother married my father, she felt attracted by the Catholic faith, and she was instructed in the truths of the faith by an excellent Irish priest, Father Bernard McKevitt, who was pastor of my father's parish, Assumption of the Blessed Virgin Mary Parish in Richland Center, Wisconsin. My mother knew the Catholic faith in depth, and she played a decisive role in transmitting it to my brothers and sisters, and to me as well. Having witnessed in my childhood the extent of her knowledge and her staunch practice of the faith, I was surprised when I learned that she had not always been Catholic. She herself, to her dying day, praised Father McKevitt for the way in which he had prepared her to enter into full communion with the Catholic faith. She always expressed also a deep gratitude for her parents' Christian faith, which had prepared her to find the fullness of that faith in the Catholic Church.

Through my father, our household was imbued with a sound Irish spirituality. The predominant feature in our home was devotion to the Sacred Heart of Jesus, which was very strongly united with Eucharistic devotion and also devotion to the Blessed Virgin, especially under her title of Our Lady of Lourdes. My parents loved the Church, and this love was manifested especially by their respect for the pastor and for the other priests of the parish. It was thanks to my parents that I began to understand the mystery of the priesthood. I was especially fond of our pastor, Father Owen Mitchell, Father McKevitt's successor, who also came from Ireland. He was the first priest to have a strong influence on my vocation, and I will always owe him a great debt of gratitude for it.

In our parish there was also a rather large number of apostolic women religious who taught at the parochial school. My parents highly respected them. I can say that as soon as I came into contact with the Sisters, I found in them an extension of my parents' love.

Do you mean that the catechism was not simplistic? That it was not just a catalogue of propositions to learn by heart?

Not at all: the definitions and formulas to be learned are rich and foster in-depth reflection on the realities of the faith. The catechism helped me to discover the profound meaning of the mysteries of the faith.

When I was a young priest, religious education was often no more than an exercise in valuing oneself, in valuing others, and in learning to live in harmony. But one cannot properly esteem oneself or others or learn to live in common without sound doctrine and a life of prayer, and especially not without the liturgy that forms us, which profoundly shapes our personal identity and our relationships with others.

Later on, I recognized more fully the serious ambiguities in the new catechetical teaching methods developed from the Sixties on: an attenuated teaching about God and His plan for human life, together with an excessive anthropocentrism, emphasizing the individual, his freedom, his feelings, and his social relations, which led often to wrong ways of living. One corollary of this catechetical method that emphasized the human individual at the expense of God was the degradation of the sexual identity of persons. In this view, the whole of reality is centered on the ego, apart from all transcendence, whereas truth and meaning are found only in the Lord and in a relationship with Him. The principle of the source of truth and meaning affects profoundly our life with others. What I experience with my brethren relates to this principle. Only through God's law, therefore, can I understand myself, the meaning of the world and of life itself, and only through God's law can I live a good life in love of neighbor.

Let us go back to your rural childhood. You said that you had bene-fited from a good primary school. Do you think that relating to cre-ation in the everyday life of a farmer's child is a plus, an aid in intellectual development that teaches the meaning of effort and hard work?

Absolutely. I remember that, when I was a child, I wanted to live like the children in the town, in other words, not to have to tend the animals or to do all the chores on the farm. Since then I have come to understand the benefits of the direct contact with nature, of all the effort it takes to harvest vegetables and fruits and also to milk the cows.

Did you bring the cows back from the pasture?

I worked with my father and my big brothers. The demand-ing reality of farm work taught me a lot. It taught me espe-cially to work at manual labor together with others and to work hard.

How did you become aware of the Lord's call? Did it happen all of a sudden or in stages?

In my family, I experienced a great love for the Lord. I then became profoundly attached to the Church. For us, life in the Church was the source of the fruitfulness of everyday routine. We knew that we were part of a family larger than our own: the parish, the diocese, and also the Universal Church. We were part of a Church that spread throughout the whole world. I remember the great filial affection of my parents for Pope Pius XII. Each of us had pictures of the Pope.

This sentiment was reinforced by the traditional form of the liturgy. For instance, I happened to meet persons who had traveled in distant lands. In those countries, they found the Mass in Latin and, thus, a universal point of contact.

In this atmosphere of faith and of unity between family life and church life, I learned to love Holy Mass, Confession, and also the various devotions, which incidentally are a very important part of our life of faith. We had a great devotion to the Sacred Heart. In our parish, we were also very devoted to Our Lady of Sorrows, and we concluded every Friday with the prayer of the Seven Sorrows of Our Lady, adoration, and Benediction of the Blessed Sacrament. Our pastor at that time was the same age as my father, and I understood very quickly that, without a priest, there was neither Eucharist nor Confession, and very early on I felt a great attraction to the priesthood.

How old were you then?

Around eight. My parents did not force me. But they did encourage me, because they thought that if God calls, it is necessary to respond and to do His will. They were very happy with my vocation.

When I was seven years old, the doctors discovered that my father had a brain tumor. His condition worsened during a year of great sufferings, and he died when I had just turned eight. During that year, my father could no longer work, and he rested at home. The priest came every week to hear his Confession and give him Holy Communion. These visits of the priest to my father left a lasting impression on me.

When he arrived with the Blessed Sacrament, we all welcomed him with lighted candles, and we preceded him, in a silent procession, to my father's room. We used to leave the room while he made his Confession, then we would return when he received Holy Communion. In this way, I was a privileged witness of his faith and his love for the Holy Eucharist. Then the priest stayed with us for a while to speak to us and console us. This very intense experience affected me deeply.

Through your family and your parish life, you became acquainted at a very early age with the Church at the ground level. How would you define the Church?

For me, the definition of the Church is very simple.

The Church is Christ living among us; she is the glorified Christ Who calls us and gathers us. Through His ministers, He teaches us the truths of the faith, He nourishes us by the sacraments, prayer, and devotion. He governs us by the Christian virtues.

What I am telling you is simple, but we see in the Gospel that when He started His public life, the Lord immediately called the Twelve and formed a community. He taught and worked miracles. He educated His followers and made them grow. During the Last Supper, He instituted the sacrament of the Eucharist as the reality of His sacrifice always present in His Church to purify us and enliven us.

How did you enter the seminary?

I can say that my family and the school helped me to grow in the priestly vocation. When I was fourteen, I told my mother about my desire to enter the diocesan minor seminary, and she agreed to send me there and to make the financial sacrifice that it entailed. After finishing elementary school in May 1962, in September of the same year I entered the diocesan minor seminary, Holy Cross Seminary in La Crosse, Wisconsin, with my mother's blessing and the recommendation of my pastor. Two other boys from my parish entered at the same time I did. That year there were eighty-four of us new students at the minor seminary: forty-two from my diocese and forty-two from other dioceses that had no minor seminary.

The minor seminary was a great grace for me. Some very good professors provided us with high-quality academic instruction; we led a life of prayer, combined with strict discipline and fine moral formation. We started the very first day with a spiritual retreat, and my spiritual director gave me *The Story of a Soul* by Saint Thérèse of Lisieux to read. I must say that this book is still the source book for my spiritual life.

The diocesan priests who looked after us gave us excellent example. They really were fathers. Obviously, the purpose of the very strict discipline at the minor seminary was the good of the young seminarians. The spiritual formation program was adapted to our age. It helped us to enter into a deeper prayer life, and it accustomed us to various spiritual practices. The Sacred Liturgy was the heart of the life at the seminary, and it was celebrated with much dignity and beauty. Those years spent at the minor seminary, from age fourteen to twenty, were for me a great gift. They helped me to understand in depth my vocation and to respond to it as was necessary.

What was the atmosphere in the Church at that time?

At that time, there was a feeling of serenity and confidence in the Church. When I was a young man, I felt a lively admiration and gratitude for the good order and richness that the life of the Church brought about. In the autumn of the year in which I entered the minor seminary, the first session of the Second Vatican Ecumenical Council began. As the sessions of the Council unfolded, an ever more strident critique of various aspects of Church life made itself heard. This was troubling. Perhaps the effects of this criticism were felt most intensely in the Sacred Liturgy. When I entered the minor seminary, every seminarian received a copy of the *Liber Usualis*. Much attention was paid to learning the proper chants for each Sunday and for the feast days. The priest in charge of Sacred Music also taught us a repertoire of polyphonic choral works. The seminary had a fine organ, which greatly increased the solemnity and the beauty of the liturgical rites. Toward the end of the Council, they very abruptly set aside the beautiful Sacred Music, which was replaced by modern music accompanied by guitar and percussion, instead of the organ. Most of the modern music was banal and sentimental. The period of experimentation in the Sacred Liturgy had begun. It led to a large number of abuses, which considerably undermined the sacred character of the liturgical action.

The changes introduced into the Sacred Liturgy were accompanied by a collapse of discipline in the seminaries and by changes introduced into the course of studies that weakened the classical character of the education that had been provided until that time. From time to time, they invited so-called experts on the Council to make presentations at the seminary. Some of these presentations betrayed a serious lack of respect for the life of the Church as it was prior to the Council and went so far as to call into question the constant teaching of the Church in matters of faith and morals.

What impressions did you have of Vatican Council II? How was that event perceived?

The beginnings of the Council were met with great enthusiasm. As far as I was concerned, at least, I considered the Council as an extraordinary way of sharing the great richness of the life and practice of the Church. The Council was viewed very positively, even though there were already some priests who began to call into question the common notion of the Council that emphasized the continuity of the Council with earlier councils and with the organic life of the Church until then. Nevertheless, there was generally a strong feeling of confidence in what the Council was going to accomplish.

As the Council unfolded, and as the various reforms that it had ordered were introduced, a certain sense of disorientation came to light. Some Church practices, for example, some devotions such as Eucharistic adoration and making visits to the Blessed Sacrament, which had done so much to nourish our faith in the Lord and our love for Him, were ridiculed and soon abandoned. Many radical changes in the life of the Church were introduced in the name of "the spirit of the Council". The Rite of Holy Mass, for example, was radically changed. Priestly and religious life and discipline, which had been so strong during my childhood, were diminished. Many of the priests with whom I was acquainted and many religious abandoned their vocation. The apostolic

women religious abandoned their habit and left their traditional apostolates of education and caring for the sick. The
number of vocations began to decline very quickly. At the
same time, attendance at Sunday Mass, and religious fervor
in general, declined. People developed a sense that many
aspects of the faith and of religious practice were now de-
batable and subject to private judgment. One of the most
shocking manifestations of this phenomenon was the loss
of the Eucharistic faith that had been so strong during my
childhood. An erroneous notion of conscience developed,
with disastrous effects in the moral life of Catholics. A sense
of assurance about life, which until then had been common
in the Church, was rather quickly replaced by a sense of
unpredictability, questioning, doubt, and experimentation.
Instead of trying to apply a remedy to this situation, there
seemed to be a sort of fascination with calling everything
into question.

*Did people already notice the difficulties that we know so well to-
day?*

In retrospect, I realize that the serious difficulties throughout
the Church today were already present, at least in the embry-
onic state, during those years. The hermeneutic of discontinuity or rupture, which Pope Benedict XVI described during his Christmas greetings to the Curia in 2005, instilled an
erroneous view of the Church. This view was accompanied
by a naïve approach to a culture that was rapidly evolving
toward total secularization, so that this secularization was
able to penetrate into the very life of the Church.

What was your ministry as a priest?

Right after my ordination, on June 29, 1975, I was appointed parochial vicar, or assistant pastor, of the cathedral parish of my diocese. At the cathedral, four Masses were celebrated every day of the week, and six on Sunday. It was also a center for the sacrament of Confession. Although in many parishes the practice of regular Confession had been abandoned, at the cathedral many hours for hearing Confessions were scheduled every week. As time went on, I realized that fewer and fewer of the faithful were going to Confession, because of a widespread feeling in the Church that regular Confession was no longer appropriate.

The two priests who were in charge of the cathedral asked me to dedicate myself more particularly to the Catholic school. After two years, the bishop asked me to teach catechism at the Catholic high school, while keeping my position as assistant at the parish. Teaching children in the Catholic elementary and high schools, I discovered that many of their families were not attending Sunday Mass, did not go to Confession regularly, and at home had little or no prayer life. What shocked me probably the most was the religious illiteracy of many children who otherwise were intelligent and well trained. I recall one incident: in a religion course for juniors in high school, most of whom had gone to Catholic schools for about eleven years, I referred to the Fifth Commandment. When one of the students raised her hand to ask what the Fifth Commandment was, I asked the other students to help her. Not one of them knew the Fifth Commandment. They did not know the sacraments, and so on. I never had any doubt about the seriousness of the duty incumbent on me to teach the catechism in depth as far as possible. One of the main difficulties was the lack of reliable catechetical texts. Moreover, the guidelines given by so-called professional catechists were far from helpful.

The first five years of my priestly ministry were a time of intense pastoral activity. I can say frankly that those five years truly strengthened my priestly vocation, thanks to the priests with whom I was working. I often recall with joy the events of those first years of my priestly ministry.

You are a canonist; where did you get this appreciation for the law?

To be perfectly frank, it was under orders from my bishop that I started, in September 1980, to study canon law, which, I must say, I did not find particularly attractive. In fact, I wanted to continue my studies in theology. The Eighties were not an easy time to study canon law. A certain antinomianism was very widespread in the Church, and the 1917 Code of Canon Law was being revised. Some priests were surprised that I should be studying something that they thought the Church had eliminated.

I was blessed to have excellent professors in the Faculty of Canon Law at the Pontifical Gregorian University. One of them in particular, Father Ignacio Gordon, S.J., took a special interest in me, and he encouraged me very much by helping me in several ways to understand the importance of the Church's discipline. At the beginning of my studies, I greatly missed teaching children and young people, which until then had been such an important part of my priestly life. Father Gordon saw that I needed to be encouraged to study canon law. With his help, and with that of other professors and classmates, I started to enjoy canon law profoundly, and even today, I enjoy studying questions related to it.

How were you called to the episcopate?

In September 1989, I was called back from my diocese to serve as defender of the bond at the Supreme Tribunal of the Apostolic Signatura. I remained there until February 1995. In early December 1994, the Secretary of the Apostolic Signatura, then-Archbishop Zenon Grocholewski, came into my office to tell me that the Prefect, Cardinal Gilberto Agustoni, wanted to see me right away. It was unusual to converse directly with the Prefect, and I was afraid that somehow or other I had made a mistake in my work, particularly in reference to certain difficult cases concerning the suppression of parishes in the United States. When I went into his office, the Prefect informed me immediately that the Holy Father, Pope John Paul II, had appointed me Bishop of La Crosse, my home diocese. I was stunned, literally speechless. He immediately added that this matter had received all due consideration and that I must not have any doubts or fears. I will always remember what he said: The cross that you will have to carry interiorly will always be heavier than the one you will carry exteriorly. He asked me to go back to my office to write a letter to the Holy Father in which I would accept the office of Bishop of La Crosse. So I went back, but for a while I could not write anything. I was overwhelmed by a sense of the weight of the responsibility of a bishop. I prayed and regained my serenity as well as the confidence that if God was calling me to accept this new and much weightier responsibility in the Church, then I had to entrust myself to the help of His grace.

On January 6, 1995, I was ordained a bishop by Pope John Paul II. After completing my work at the Apostolic Signatura, I returned to my diocese, where I was installed as the bishop on February 22, 1995. I spent almost nine years as Bishop of La Crosse. Those were years of intense pastoral activity, under the firm, profound direction of Pope John Paul II. One of the biggest challenges was promoting vocations to the priestly and consecrated life. There was also the need to address all the aspects of the new evangelization to which Pope John Paul II was insistently calling the Church.

In your opinion, what qualities should a bishop develop?

It seems to me that the most important virtues for a bishop to develop are humility and confidence. Humility allows him to recognize that in all things he is a successor of the Apostles and that he must carry out his duties in obedience to Christ and to the Vicar of Christ on earth, the Roman Pontiff. Confidence enables him to go forward in the trying circumstances of the present time, knowing that the Lord is the one who will make fruitful the feeble efforts of the bishop on behalf of all his faithful.

In a special way, from the very beginning of my episcopal ministry, I had a very strong sense that it was important for me to devote all my fatherly attention to the priests and seminarians as well as to those who were called to the priesthood but had not yet entered the seminary. The bishop has pastoral responsibility for the whole flock of his diocese, but it will not be possible for him to perform his duties successfully if he does not have a large number of worthy priests to help him. Sometimes I have been criticized because I did not pay enough attention to the laity. My response has been that my pastoral concern for the lay faithful was precisely what led me to devote so much attention to those who would then be directly at their service as priests. But of course I spent a lot of time on matters affecting the laity. I often met with them, either individually or in groups.

In December 2003, I was transferred from the Diocese of La Crosse to the Archdiocese of Saint Louis, Missouri. I was installed there on January 26, 2004. One of my greatest joys in the Archdiocese of Saint Louis was Kenrick-Glennon Seminary. I considered it the real heart of the archdiocese, and every week I tried to attend directly to the life of the seminary. The archdiocese was greatly blessed to have many excellent priestly vocations. The presence of the seminary in the archdiocese was a great help for the young men who were discerning their vocation.

What were the biggest difficulties confronting you in your episcopal ministry?

It was the invasive secularization of the culture, which unfortunately had also entered into the life of the Church. Because catechesis had been dangerously impoverished in its content for several decades, it prevented the faithful from giving witness in the culture as Christians. The formation of the seminarians, too, had been weakened and had lost its bearings, already at the time when I was in seminary. The priests therefore often found themselves, without any fault on their part, ill prepared to teach and to form others as they ought to have. There were also some older priests who had received a solid doctrinal formation and a solid discipline that they had been led to call into question in the name of the alleged "spirit of the Council". In moral questions, proportionalism and consequentialism led some to call into question the moral teaching of the Church and, in certain cases, the natural moral law.

They say that nowadays many candidates refuse the episcopal office for fear of being unable to take on that task; is this common?

I have no way of knowing how many candidates to the episcopacy refuse the Holy Father's call to accept the episcopal office. I have been acquainted with one or two candidates who refused the Holy Father's appointment. In both cases, the candidates did not feel prepared to face the attacks that the secular culture, especially the mass media, launches against the Church or the internal conflicts of the Church, caused by a lack of sound doctrine and discipline.

What real freedom does a bishop have? Is it not limited by administrative structures at the diocesan or national level (bishops' conference)? Can he really act?

The diocesan bishop is, by divine mandate, the first teacher of the faith in his diocese, the first liturgist, and the first pastor. The diocesan administrative structures and the bishops' conference can in no way take from the bishop his responsibility in matters concerned with teaching the faith, his personal offering of the Sacred Liturgy, and the fact that he must see to it that the liturgy is celebrated in a worthy manner in his diocese. The administrative structures are designed to help the bishop. In some matters, for example, in the extraordinary administration of temporal goods, he can act only under certain conditions. Some consultative and deliberative bodies are also normative for the diocese, but they do not diminish at all the responsibility incumbent on the bishop: that of governing his flock with wisdom and fortitude. In particular, he must keep in mind that the office of diocesan bishop is of divine right; the bishops' conference is a structure of positive ecclesiastical law. It is designed to help the bishops in the pastoral care of their flock, but it is not a national corporation of bishops that dictates to them what they must do and controls them. Similarly, the bishops' conference cannot represent the bishops of a territory on the sole authority of the conference.

And then you were called to Rome by Benedict XVI. What sort of an experience was that? Was it difficult for you to leave your diocese?

It was especially painful for me to leave the Archdiocese of Saint Louis, where I had been Archbishop for only four and a half years. When I was appointed Archbishop of Saint Louis, I did not know very much about that archdiocese. When I started to minister to it, I very quickly learned to love it. There are many devout Catholic individuals and families who pray for their Archbishop, support him, and help him. The archdiocese is also blessed to have its own seminary. When I was Archbishop, it was a special source of joy to direct the work of supporting priestly vocations and to form future priests at the seminary. During the years that I spent in Saint Louis, we were blessed with many excellent priestly vocations. I became well acquainted with a large number of pious, very intelligent, and selfless young men who had answered Christ's call: "Follow me!"

You were appointed Prefect of the Supreme Tribunal of the Apostolic Signatura. What did your work consist of?

I already knew very well the mission of the Supreme Tribunal of the Apostolic Signatura. I had had the privilege of serving there as defender of the bond from September 1989 to February 1995, when I began my service as Bishop of La Crosse. It was a great honor to be appointed Prefect of the Apostolic Signatura, an honor of which I did not feel worthy. At the Apostolic Signatura, I found a well-trained team that was united and very devoted. It was not difficult for me to return to the service that the Apostolic Signatura provides for the Universal Church and to dedicate myself to it.

In the Church, canon law protects and fosters holy things like the sacraments and the teaching of the faith, without forgetting just relations between the faithful and their pastors as well as among the faithful themselves. The task of the tribunal of the Apostolic Signatura, as the supreme tribunal and bureau of justice, is to assure a minimum of good order that allows the performance of "more glorious" tasks in the Church, such as the liturgy and the proclamation of the faith. There is no peace in the ecclesial body without justice.

Are you far removed from the life of the average Christian when you work in the Vatican?

Not at all, nothing of the sort. At the Apostolic Signatura, I had a very broad knowledge of what is happening in the world. The questions, the dossiers that we studied, are quite representative of the life of people today, of their trials and sufferings. It is impossible to do real work in the Roman Curia without a strong sense of the salvation of souls. It is a very beautiful thing to work in the service of the Roman Curia. I regret very much the caricatures of it: a group of old men living in an unreal world or a group of ambitious priests for whom the spiritual good of the faithful is of no importance.

When one is acquainted with the Vatican administration, one is struck by its reduced size: so few persons to manage thousands of bishops, hundreds of thousands of priests, a billion faithful. How is it possible?

It is true that the Roman Curia provides for the Church throughout the world a wide-ranging service, even though the resources of the various departments or dicasteries of the Roman Curia are rather slight. The Apostolic Signatura, for example, although it deals with more than a thousand tribunals worldwide and has the responsibility for final judgments in administrative cases in which there is an alleged violation of ecclesiastical law, has in all only fourteen members on its staff, including the two gentlemen who function as receptionists and take care of a number of subsidiary tasks. How is it possible for so few persons to accomplish so much? First of all, according to my experience of it, those who have responsibility in the various offices display great devotion. They are not content to do the work of the dicastery during office hours but also work at home. Furthermore, the Church is an organic body in which a very rich tradition that has been uninterrupted since the time of the Apostles provides its inspiration and guidance to the work, which makes it proceed more quickly and much more calmly.

There has been a lot of talk about scandals in the Vatican . . . Have we really returned to the time of Pope Borgia?

In my opinion, we certainly have not gone back to the moral situation in the time of Pope Alexander VI Borgia. Surely, some members of the Roman Curia or some officials of the State of the Vatican have seriously failed in their duty and, in some cases, have even been involved in criminal activities; but they are few in number. Most of the clerics, consecrated religious, and lay faithful who are in the service of the Roman Curia and Vatican City State are faithful to the duties of their state in life, and they serve in an exemplary fashion the Apostolic See or the State of the Vatican. I am proud to have been in the service of the Roman Curia, even at a time when some scandals surfaced because of the failings and sins of certain individuals.

In Rome, a new era is beginning with the election of Pope Francis and his style of governing, which is so different from that of Pope Benedict XVI. You gave up your positions of responsibility in 2014: Do you have any regrets, anything that you would have liked to accomplish?

Of course, it was very difficult for me to leave the service of the Supreme Tribunal of the Apostolic Signatura. It was a work for which I was well prepared by my studies and experience. Moreover, the personnel of the Apostolic Signatura are very united. I felt close to all the members of my team. Of course, there were other things that I had hoped to accomplish, if I had had more time as Prefect. Be that as it may, I entrust myself to Divine Providence, and therefore I am happy to be at the service of the Sovereign Military Order of Malta, as Cardinal Patron of the Order.

PART TWO

The Church and the World in Crisis

They say that the contemporary Church is in crisis, but is this really a new phenomenon? Doesn't the Church regularly experience similar situations?

At various times in her history, the Church has been in a situation similar to the one today. In fact, in every age the Church will find herself in conflict with the world and its way of thinking and acting. Our Lord Jesus Christ made that very clear to us, both by His teaching and by the example of His own public ministry, His sufferings and death on the cross. He told us that if we wanted to follow Him, we had to take up our cross each day. Just think of His glorious disciples over the course of the Christian centuries who were confessors of the faith or martyrs. Think of the faithful Christians such as Saint Polycarp or Saint Agatha at the time of the Roman persecutions, or Saint John Fisher and Saint Thomas More during the persecution of the Church under King Henry VIII of England, or again of Saint Charles Lwanga and his companions in nineteenth-century Uganda, who preferred to undergo a martyr's death rather than to betray Christ by indulging in gravely disordered acts with the corrupt King Mwanga.

Hasn't the crisis in society, the crisis of values in general, affected the Church?

The crisis of the Church is identified with 1968, the year of the revolution started by Parisian students against all forms of authority. And therefore this crisis was unleashed by a false understanding of the relation between faith and culture.

Even today, I hear bishops and theologians recalling the speech with which Saint John XXIII opened the Council, the Address *Gaudet Mater Ecclesia*, in which he spoke about the relation between culture and faith, and they interpret this speech as an invitation to adapt the faith to the culture. And there was a widespread feeling that the whole life of the Church before the Council was worthless, that it was necessary to create a new Church in order to live in a world that had changed a lot. Yes, the world has changed, but the faith is the rock that remains and allows us to navigate the troubled waters of today's world.

But unfortunately we have lost the sense of the great gift of the faith, the sense of what the Church is and the sense of Tradition. I was very much inspired by the Address of Pope Benedict XVI to the Curia, on the occasion of the Solemnity of the Nativity of the Lord in 2005. In it, he explained how to interpret the conciliar reforms by using two formulas, contrasting "the hermeneutic of discontinuity and rupture" with "the hermeneutic of reform in continuity".

Let us make a clean slate of the past . . .

Yes, that's right, everything from the past must be abolished and replaced by something new. And then, on the other hand, Pope Benedict mentioned the hermeneutic of reform in continuity. The one Church of Christ never changes, and eternal truths endure.

In my childhood, they taught me that the life of the Church develops organically, that the centuries hand down to us the truths of the faith in an uninterrupted chain, according to the principle that the new sprouts spring from the old trunk.

We met with the same revolutionary spirit in the liturgy . . .

I remember that in the years after 1968, I attended liturgical celebrations that had retained almost nothing of what could be a Mass. I had gone to the Netherlands, at that time, and witnessed a Mass in which the priest arrived in civilian clothing. The whole celebration was totally unrecognizable as a Holy Mass.

Blessed Paul VI, in his famous homily on the Solemnity of Saints Peter and Paul in 1972, declared that the smoke of Satan had entered into the sanctuary of the Church. Later, Pope John Paul II and then Pope Benedict XVI did much by their teachings to reestablish liturgical continuity.

In your opinion, is the decline in practice of the faith in so-called developed countries connected to this desire to create a new man, liberated from the past by the principle of dialectic, which says that the past must necessarily be opposed to the dynamic of progress?

During the years after 1968, I noted a drop in attendance at Sunday Mass. Catholics believed less and less in the presence of Christ in the Eucharist, the number of divorces increased, the catechism largely lost its substance, many priests and consecrated religious abandoned their priestly or religious state. The Sixties reaction was libertarian: "It is forbidden to forbid!" In reality, life also needs a juridical form, in the sense of a just relation with God and neighbor.

That is true, Your Eminence, but someone might object that these people had been formed before the Council . . .

I think that in the Fifties and Sixties, people to a large extent had already lost the sense of handing on the faith. They assumed too much that the faith and the practice of it were things acquired once and for all. At the same time, a very strong but erroneous feeling of human progress developed, which refused to acknowledge that God is the source of all that we have and that we are only the stewards, and not the masters, of creation and history. This made it difficult to receive God's gift, and the truths of the faith were no longer accepted with the heart of a child.

This reflected the thought of the new era, in which the center of intellectual, spiritual, and moral life, and also of scientific discoveries and technological advances, which a short time before had been God, was now the individual subject. More and more man became his own idol, making his subjective impressions the judge of good and evil. Very often he has forgotten or denied the sense of mystery, and therefore he has no longer been able to marvel at it. Along with mystery, the sense of the faith and of the sacred has gradually faded. At the same time, people have suffered cruelly from a lack of formation and, at best, have kept up a rootless formalism, whether in their human relations or in their liturgical practice.

The lay people, living in an increasingly secularized world that is more and more foreign to the sacred, very often have not received from the clergy the word that they needed.

Families, and even priests and consecrated religious, have gradually abandoned devotion and the meaning of the life of the Church.

Do you mean that material progress can stifle the growth of the interior life?

Exactly. There were many priestly and religious vocations in the aftermath of World War II because people had gone through terrible trials that had caused their faith to mature. But rather quickly the increase subsided, and that must be connected in part with the rapid recovery of Europe after its devastation. It is true that the West went through a period of very strong economic development, leading to a time of prosperity unknown until then.

The extraordinary development of technology revived the old pride, which soon brought about the eclipse of God in men's minds. From then on, the Catholic faith, its dogmas, rites, and devotions, appeared to be a useless constraint left over from another age, flowery, medieval legends for children and the elderly. Given over entirely to their pride, man and modern society turned their back on their past and their history. "Let us make a clean slate of the past": you see how the adolescent slogan of the Revolution and of the Fall was revived.

The infamous culture of death was indeed already present. Did Marxism and unbridled capitalism accelerate the process set in motion by the French Revolution?

In modern thought, reality is limited to matter and man's action on it. And therefore it has radically distanced itself from the One Who alone provides the key for interpreting the universe—God, Who is the Alpha and the Omega of history.

You are right to say that the process set in motion by the French Revolution has continued its course unbridled in recent decades. The grand capitalism of those who adore mammon, the ideologies that claimed to liberate man and society, while amputating their spiritual dimension and turning God into a kind of "opium", are nothing but new forms of slavery. All who have turned away from Christ have seen that Satan is a bloody tyrant.

We can say then that 1968 was not the beginning of a crisis, but a step in the deconstruction of man's relations with God . . .

We might say that a tumor grew imperceptibly during the Fifties and Sixties and that it was revealed at the end of a period of apparent progress and well-being.

Many Catholic families today are confronted with the aggressions of the liberal mind. The internet brings the best and the worst into the home. The tabernacle of television, which had already greatly contributed to the weakening of faith and the family atmosphere, finds a powerful assistant in the internet, with its various technological derivatives such as tablets and iPhones. How do you react to this?

All the means of social communication, which are developing more and more, are a great gift to help us lead a more human and more Christian life. Unfortunately, it is all too easy for us not to regard them as tools at the service of a virtuous life and of the supreme good of love of God and of neighbor; thus we become slaves to these means of communication, and our human and Christian character diminishes. Think, for example, of someone who spends hours in front of his computer screen and yet does not have the time to relate responsibly within his family or at work. This situation is so absurd that members of the same family even send each other text messages while they are under the same roof. Some individuals tell me that they prefer to send text messages rather than to communicate directly.

We, as persons, and most especially as parents, must pay close attention to what we ourselves or our children watch on television or on the computer. While you can find on television or on the internet many nice series and important news, you find also a lot of toxic waste that undermines the moral sense of adults and corrupts children from the earliest age. The communications media are powerful, but we are their masters, not their subjects.

In the Church, too, aren't some people tempted to try at all costs to reconcile the spirit of the world with that of the Gospel? The question of married priests and of what feminists think should be the place of women in society comes to the fore . . .

It is right that the Church should encounter contemporary culture, not to make a formal compromise with it, but to bear witness to Christ, Who alone can transform a culture to make it serve the common good. Priestly celibacy, for example, makes no sense in a culture that has lost the meaning of human sexuality and, consequently, all sense of the complementarity between marriage and virginity, between the state of marriage and the state of celibacy. Similarly, the Church cannot adopt the program of radical feminism, for example, by admitting women to the ordained priesthood.

Christ's word, which the Church transmits to the culture, makes very clear the distinct gifts of man and woman, in the family as well as in the Church.

What is your reaction to the progressive disintegration of certain Protestant and Anglican communities that have espoused the spirit of secularism?

When an ecclesial community begins to compromise with the world, with an entirely secularized culture, that is the sign that it has lost its apostolic roots and, thereby, its very identity. In the Thirties, there was great pressure on Christians to accept the practice of contraception as a way of regulating births, a practice that the Church, in her uninterrupted tradition, had never accepted. Only the Roman Catholic Church remained faithful to that moral tradition. Then, in the Sixties, strong pressure was brought to bear on the Church to change her teaching, which of course she could not do. When Blessed Paul VI reaffirmed what the Church had always taught, thus contradicting the trend of the world, there was a strong reaction.

We observe situations like that whenever ecclesial communities have abandoned the apostolic teaching, for example, on the inviolability of innocent, defenseless human life, on the integrity of marriage, understood as the indissoluble union of one man and one woman that is open to new life, and on the ordained priesthood.

Do you see a difference between Europe and the United States with regard to Church life?

We are the children of Europe, and the culture of the United States is European. You know that my family, for example, is originally from Ireland.

In the United States, secularization arrived later and less violently than in Europe. We have maintained a rather strong sense of Christianity, which nevertheless, as in Europe, is at odds with the rejection of God and the culture of death.

Do you think that the crisis is behind us?

I think that the crisis is still present, and we continue to work for the re-Christianization of the United States, in the context of battles against certain governmental decisions.

The federal government is trying to reduce religious liberty, contrary to the Constitution of the United States. President Obama wants to push the Church back behind the walls of her church buildings and to prevent her from applying her law to her own hospitals and schools. He claims that the Church may not intervene on the question of abortion, of homosexuality, but that the State alone must manage these questions.

Can it be said that, for the last ten years approximately, the American episcopate has changed its tone and stands up more to defend human life, the family, and Catholic doctrine?

The bishops, as pastors of the flock, have a very important mission, which they cannot shirk. Currently, they are very united on the question of defending human life and the family. During the recent Synod on the Family, in its first assembly, the bishops of the United States were in line with the teaching of the Magisterium.

Incidentally, it is obvious that the appointment of good bishops is essential for the proclamation of the Gospel.

On this subject, they often say that it is important for the bishops to be in communion with one another. Sometimes you wonder whether the criterion of communion is merely human. I have the feeling that some are afraid of originality and interior freedom. You get the impression occasionally that the source of communion is found, not in unity of faith, but in the desire not to make waves, to go with the consensus. The more secularized we are, the less we surprise the world with the prophetic daring of our witness to the truth and the less in communion we are.

When I was Bishop of La Crosse, I took clear positions concerning respect for the liturgy and the teaching of authentic catechesis. Someone accused me of dividing the priests. I replied: "No, the priests are already divided."

I always wanted to teach as the Church teaches, in other words, according to the Magisterium of the Church, for only in that way can one work for unity. Incidentally, the bishops' conference, which is no doubt a good thing, can also create a false unity. The latter consists of always being in agreement horizontally, superficially. But the cracks appear as soon as you address basic questions. For example, I remember that in 2004 I asked Catholic politicians to make their public actions consistent with the moral law taught by the Church; otherwise it would no longer be possible for them to receive Holy Communion. It was necessary for me to address the matter because it is a scandal to violate the moral law publicly and then to approach to receive Holy Communion.

In 2004, when I was transferred from the Diocese of La Crosse to the Archdiocese of Saint Louis, some journalists reported the statements that I had made. Shortly after, during the summer meeting of the United States Conference of Catholic Bishops, there was a lively discussion on this disciplinary practice of the Church. Some of my confreres even told me that we must not punish Catholic politicians whose political activity was disordered.

As I see it, this was not about punishment but simply stating that some people were not well disposed to receive Holy Communion. One bishop then told me: "Your Excellency, you should not have said what you said, because the conference of bishops has not yet made a pronouncement on this subject." I replied that the conference of bishops should not try to replace the mission of the bishop in his own diocese, which is to govern his flock and to proclaim the faith. And I added: "Your Excellency, at the last judgment, I will appear before the Lord, and not before the conference of bishops."

I think that, unfortunately for us, we have lost the sense of the spiritual reality of the Church. Certainly, structures are important, but they must be inspired by a sound ecclesiological vision.

A French Eudist priest [of the Congregation of Jesus and Mary] who died in 2005, the Reverend Father Henri Macé, liked to say that in the Church every heresy is connected with a lack of understanding of the mystery of the Church. You might say in a way that a theological error is in the first place ecclesiological.

Exactly, moral and doctrinal errors result from an ecclesiological problem. I will also say that many difficulties that we experience in the Church come from philosophical problems. Ambiguity and confusion are the consequence.

Is the relativism that Benedict XVI spoke about the most serious danger threatening the Church?

Yes, I agree and say, with Pope Benedict XVI, that relativism—the loss of a sound metaphysics and, consequently, of a sense of an objective reality—is the greatest danger in our days. It leads to so many errors that profoundly destroy persons and society. It hinders a just relationship with God that helps us to behave responsibly toward others and in the world.

Is Islam the danger looming over this new millennium? Should the Church be afraid of it?

It is necessary for the Church, and for her members, to understand correctly what Islam is and what the Qur'an [Koran] teaches. Islam is not just another religious practice that can coexist in harmony with other religions. Islam is a religion that, according to its own interpretation, must also become the State. The Qur'an, and the authentic interpretations of it given by various experts in quranic law, is destined to govern the world. In reality, there is no place for other religions, even though they may be tolerated, as long as Islam has not succeeded in establishing its sovereignty over the nations and over the world. It is important for Christians to realize the radical differences between Islam and Christianity in matters concerning their teaching about God, about conscience, etc. If you really understand Islam, you understand that the Church really should be afraid of it.

PART THREE

A Spiritual Renewal

What is the remedy for the current situation?

We must return to our roots, to the foundations of our being, and therefore to metaphysics. It is good to go back and reflect again on the meaning of existence, of family life, of life in society and in the world. The human mind needs a realist philosophy to serve as a basis for its understanding of the mysteries of the faith. God alone is the goal of our quest, and everything must lead to Him. Contemporary man will recover from the current situation only with this theocentric perspective. And to arrive at this perspective, we must get rid of all the forms of narcissistic individualism that come from the secularized world. A life that is fruitful, renewed, and converted can be sustained only by the Sacred Liturgy, celebrated with dignity, for it offers us the riches of centuries of Church life.

At the same time, we must rediscover the meaning of family life. We must rediscover the school, founded on Christian morality. And we must learn anew the fundamental virtues of modesty, purity, and honesty so as to be able to live together in the sight of God.

From the experience of my priestly ministry, I can say that young people are thirsting to hear the truths of the faith. They want to learn to pray and to participate better in the liturgy. They live in such a secularized environment, which stifles them, whereas my generation, as I told you, was able to grow up in a Christian environment.

Often these young people have experienced the divorce of their parents and the emotional problems that ensue. They are subjected to pornography, to "liberation" from morality; they are drawn into uninhibited lives that are not fulfilling. Many are looking for true love.

But I observe also that many of these young people, who live in this world from which God is excluded, feel a great attraction to a beautiful, holy liturgy that is celebrated with the dignity that befits the Holy Sacrifice, whether in the Extraordinary Form or in the Ordinary Form of the Roman Rite, provided that there is great devotion and the sense of transcendence that indicates that we are turned toward the Lord and that the sacrifice on Calvary is being renewed.

And at the level of the Church?

The Church must rediscover her theocentric vision. We must rediscover the true meaning of the liturgy, which is a gift from God and not something that comes from us and is of our making. It is a gift from God that carries us and cleanses us from our sins, through which God teaches us to live a holy life, and it causes us to grow in faith, hope, and charity. We must discover a right relation between the faith and the culture in which we live.

Your Eminence, in your ministry you come into contact with different spiritual families, among them some new communities. These include societies of apostolic life and religious congregations, whether

*charismatic or not, Opus Dei . . . What do you think of these dif-
ferent components of the Church? In your opinion is this one of the
signs of renewal?*

It is necessary to make a distinction between forms of consecrated life, ecclesial movements, and Opus Dei, which is
a personal prelature, in other words, a jurisdiction within
the Church for those who follow the spirituality and discipline presented in the teaching of Saint Josemaría Escrivá
de Balaguer. Consecrated life is a state of life in the Church
distinct from the clerical state and from the lay state. The
various forms of consecrated life and the various institutes
of consecrated life were inspired by the Holy Spirit for the
edification of the Church. In all forms of consecrated life,
persons follow Christ more closely, especially by the pro-
fession of the evangelical counsels of poverty, chastity, and
obedience; they are therefore the source of inspiration and
strength for the clergy as well as for the laity. The ecclesial
movements provide their members with certain spiritual assistance, so that they can live their Christian life more intensely.

The important thing to understand about ecclesial movements is that they are all *in* the Universal Church and *for* the
Universal Church and in the diocese and its parishes. They
can never constitute a community parallel to the Church.
Nowadays, when the family is the target of so many attacks
by an entirely secularized culture, it is important to reinforce
the parish, which is, in the words of Pope John Paul II, "a
family of families". In this way, the Church's pastoral plan
—which is Christ living for us in the Church and, therefore, holiness of life in Christ, as Pope John Paul II taught

so forcefully in *Novo millennio ineunte*, his Apostolic Letter for the conclusion of the Great Jubilee Year 2000—can be followed faithfully.

You often address the question of the liturgy. Do you think that this is an important question?

As I just said, young people today, who grew up in a very secularized world, show a great love for the Sacred Liturgy, in which they see Christ at work for our sanctification. It is of the utmost importance that the manner of rendering divine worship should allow Christ's action to become more and more visible and tangible. Worship centered on man is a self-contradiction, and this is what led many people to stop attending Sunday Mass and other sacramental celebrations.

Is liturgical formation adequate? What aspects could be improved?

The Church is still grappling with the ravages caused by a wrong interpretation of the liturgical reform that the Fathers of the Second Vatican Ecumenical Council had desired. The violent reform of the liturgical rites, which was accompanied by encouragement of experimentation with these rites, was the cause of great damage, not only to sound liturgical practice, but also to sound faith and morals. It seems to me that one of the great legacies of the pontificate of Pope Benedict XVI is the effort that he undertook to reform the Sacred Liturgy according to the teaching of Vatican II, and not according to the alleged "spirit of the Council". He urged us forcefully with the promulgation of the *Motu proprio Summorum Pontificum* to rediscover the sense of the organic unity of the Sacred Liturgy handed down over the Christian centuries and, thereby, its transcendent reality.

You recently wrote the preface to a book on how to receive Holy Communion. What is your deep conviction on this subject?

It is clear that the way in which we receive Holy Communion expresses our faith with regard to the Sacred Host that we receive. The generalized introduction of receiving Holy Communion in the hand, even though there are precedents for it in antiquity, has led, in my experience of it, to rather casual attitudes toward the Real Presence and sometimes, even, in certain cases, harmful attitudes toward the Eucharistic Body of Christ. Similarly, the practice of receiving Holy Communion while standing does not adequately express our adoration of the Body of Christ given to us despite our unworthiness. I much prefer reception of Holy Communion on the tongue, while kneeling at the communion rail.

Some express their disappointment with the reluctance of some clerics to implement the Motu proprio Summorum Pontificum. *Might this come from a lack of understanding of what Benedict XVI said he wanted: "the mutual enrichment" of the two forms? Indeed, in order to be able to enrich each other, there still have to be two options.*

Since the reform of the Roman Rite of the Mass was so radical, the only way the two forms—the form of the rite until 1962 and the form of the postconciliar rite—can enrich each other is when it is possible for both forms of the rite to be celebrated freely and widely. Where that is happening, I have noticed that there has been a deepening of liturgical faith and piety. If the Sacred Liturgy is organic in its expressions over the course of the centuries, then we must not fear to celebrate according to the form of the Roman Rite that was in use before the Council. The catechesis of Pope Benedict XVI at the time when he promulgated *Summorum Pontificum* and also in his writings on the liturgy in general are an invaluable help for understanding the eternal beauty of the Sacred Liturgy.

How should we understand the expression "mutual enrichment"?

"Mutual enrichment" means that there are valuable elements in each of the two forms of the Roman Rite and that identifying, understanding, and cultivating these elements can help to bring about the true reform of the Sacred Liturgy.

It is not always easy for communities that practice their faith in the two forms of the Roman Rite to coexist in a diocese. How can communion between them be promoted?

I was the bishop of two dioceses in which I promoted the celebration of both forms of the Roman Rite. On the whole, the celebration of the two forms caused no difficulties. These difficulties occur when there is what I would call a liturgical ideology, which demonizes one or the other form. A tried and true liturgical catechesis and a solid formation in liturgical piety will increasingly foster the dignified celebration of the two forms of the Roman Rite.

One gets the impression that the young generations of priests have gone beyond the debates of the Sixties and are more united in their vision of the Church and the priesthood. Do you agree with this assessment?

In the relations that I have had with young priests, both as diocesan bishop and as a cardinal working in Rome, I have observed that they do not understand the sort of revolution in the Church that is identified with May 1968 and that certainly they do not take part in it. They are eager to know Tradition and to experience it. They grew up in an era when children and young people were no longer introduced to the many riches of the faith and of the Church's practice and when a large part of the wealth of tradition had been abandoned, while at the same time they suffered from the moral bankruptcy of an entirely secularized society.

The Christian communities in Africa and Asia are flourishing. Will the future of the Church be on those young continents? Has the Church in the West "seen its day"?

The young Churches of Africa and Asia often display some of the energy and commitment of the first evangelization. From this perspective, they should inspire the Church in the West to undertake the New Evangelization to which Blessed Paul VI and Saint John Paul II so constantly exhorted us and which was the subject matter of their teaching. The Church never ends, wherever she may be in the world, because Christ, Who is faithful to His promises, always remains with the Church, in every place and until the end of the world. Where the Church seems to be disappearing, she must dedicate herself once more to the teaching of the faith, to adoration and prayer, and to a virtuous life, with renewed energy and commitment. Indeed, even though in many respects the Church in the West may seem to be near death, there are also many signs of a new blossoming of the faith, which we must encourage and in which we must take part. During visits that I have made to some very secularized countries of Europe, in which attendance at Sunday Mass and participation in the life of the Church have declined considerably, I have never failed to find faithful persons and families and young priests and seminarians who love the Church, her teaching, her Sacred Liturgy, and her discipline.

PART FOUR

Proclaiming the Gospel of Life

Your Eminence, when did you first begin to take to heart a concern for defending the life of the weakest? Is there an incident that made you particularly sensitive to this serious question?

I grew up in a world that was very sensitive to the most helpless. I remember the concern that we had in our family for the elderly, the sick. In my childhood, I was acquainted with persons with disabilities and learned from my parents the great respect that we should have for those who are frail. My father had only one sister, and she had Down syndrome. Our family always paid her a lot of attention.

On this subject, my mother told me that while she was expecting me she had suffered from a serious illness. She had to stay in the hospital for several weeks. This was in 1948. The doctor suggested that my mother have an abortion. He told her: "You already have five children, it is important for you to be in good health so as to take care of them." My parents refused. I should explain that the doctor was not Catholic. My parents told him that they believed in God and that Christ would give them the necessary help. My mother gave birth to me, and everything went well. I was therefore quite touched by this question of defending human life, because I could very well have been killed.

During the years of my childhood, abortion was a rare practice. When I was a young man, I experienced the legalization of abortion with the Supreme Court decision *Roe versus Wade* in 1973. After that came the rise in the number of abortions. Now there are more than a million abortions every year in the United States. Every day, I think of each life that is destroyed, irrevocably lost, by human agency. In my opinion, this situation cannot continue. With the arrival of abortion, society has experienced an increase in violence. The murder of the smallest and most defenseless human beings is the root of social violence. Now, some people say that people with serious illnesses or the elderly are useless. That is truly horrible. You can see the profoundly selfish, individualistic logic that is behind this view of a human being and his dignity.

You must have appreciated very much the teaching of Pope John Paul II about the inviolable worth of every human life, about the beauty and greatness of the family.

Yes, Saint John Paul II is the great apostle of life. The Encyclical *Evangelium vitae* is always the point of reference for me on questions about protecting and promoting human life. At the beginning of his pontificate, with great wisdom, for four years, he devoted his Wednesday audiences to an explanation of *Humanae vitae*. I am convinced that the root of the ferocious attack against life today is the distortion of the sexual act by contraception, the idea that one can separate the conjugal act from the possible procreation of new life. That is impossible, because the conjugal act is by nature procreative. The intimate union of spouses does not necessarily lead to the gift of life, but it must be open to life. The mutual total gift of the spouses includes also the reality that they give their fertility to one another, the fantastic power to cooperate with God in the creation of a new life. As I already noted, in the Thirties, the Anglican communities accepted contraception. In the years that followed, this was also the case with other separated Christian communities, until the Sixties, when pressures within and outside the Catholic Church were brought to bear on her to authorize contraception. But Blessed Paul VI, with the courage of a true pastor, proclaimed once again the Gospel of life against contraception. In continuity with the Magisterium of Blessed Paul VI, Pope Benedict XVI provides an excellent teaching in *Caritas in veritate*: one cannot understand human development correctly without the Encyclical *Humanae vitae*.

What did you do in the dioceses of which you were bishop to facilitate greater awareness of the inviolability of human life from conception until natural death? With regard to the priests, the faithful, the ecclesial movements, prayer, and grass-roots activity?

I devoted many of my homilies to respect for the inviolability of innocent human life. At the same time, I insisted on the urgency of this proclamation by catechesis and the formation of catechists. Of course, it took a lot of work to get the Catholic schools to adopt again in its entirety the teaching of the Church about life and family.

We organized public pro-life prayer vigils, especially in front of clinics where they performed abortions or on the sad anniversary of the Supreme Court decision legalizing abortion.

In my different dioceses, I organized days on which to celebrate the magnificent Encyclical by Saint John Paul II, *Evangelium vitae*, and I invited experts in moral theology to speak to us about the pro-life teaching of Pope John Paul II.

I often met with the seminarians and priests to remind them insistently that the role of pastors of the flock is to protect the weakest, who are the defenseless little ones. In parallel with this pastoral activity, a vast movement developed in the schools: young people formed associations to promote respect for the life of the little preborn children and the life of persons with disabilities, seriously ill or elderly persons, for even then we had sensed that another attack against life was coming: euthanasia.

How did the parishes implement your directives concerning the battle to be fought?

I must say that the parishes received them very well. In each one, there was a good group of leaders, and, among the faithful generally, there was very strong support for the pro-life movement. There were of course some who opposed it, but fortunately, they were relatively rare. In the Archdiocese of Saint Louis, the pro-life movement was already well developed. When the Supreme Court ruled to legalize abortion, the Archbishop at the time, Cardinal John J. Carberry, immediately formed an archdiocesan committee to promote life and opened a special pro-life office. He insisted that in every parish persons be delegated to report to the Archbishop's chancery on the pro-life cause. Every year in Saint Louis there is a big pro-life conference with many presentations and with opportunities for people to become acquainted with good books and different pro-life organizations. Incidentally, this conference meets with great success. In the United States, young people are very sensitive to the pro-life movement. On the occasion of the March for Life in Washington, D.C., one young man put it this way: "I was born in 1975, and I have to thank my parents for having allowed me to be born." The young people are aware that every life is in danger before birth.

If there was any resistance, what was your method of winning hearts for this noble cause?

There was real resistance from public opinion, from institutions and hospitals that perform abortions, and from very combative feminist groups that are militantly in favor of a woman's right to have control of her body and therefore to choose abortion. These pro-choice groups claim a pseudo-freedom of choice, which they pit against the right to life.

My response to the faithful who might have been discouraged by the violence of the opposition could be summarized as follows: we must always bear witness, in season and out of season. When the moment comes, the Lord, Who is the master of time, will make this witness fruitful. It does not matter that it was poorly received.

On the contrary: the strongest witness must be given when the resistance is strongest. The devil, of course, wants to discourage us; he tries to sow doubt in our minds about defending human life publicly. And he subtly tempts us to remain silent, to mute our conscience, to tell ourselves that we are personally against abortion but do not have to express our faith and moral convictions in public.

We are citizens of our country, and our duty to society is to witness to the moral law, which is the prerequisite for peace in our life together.

I know very well that this is difficult today. But we do not choose the time in which God asks us to live, and we must accept the fact.

Have you met people who had difficulty understanding the Church's message about defending life?

I have received a number of letters that contained abusive language. The writers accused me of hypocrisy and cruelty, of belonging to another era . . .

Some individuals came to see me to communicate their arguments to me. My duty was to receive them with patience and serenity, while calmly presenting the teaching of the Church. Occasionally, some confrontations were difficult. I always had the conviction that clear, calm testimony would leave in the hostile person's soul a seed that will someday bear fruit.

When I was created a cardinal, I received a letter from a Catholic in the Diocese of La Crosse who until then had violently opposed my conviction on this subject. He told me that, with the passage of time, he had come to understand the Church's position, and he asked my forgiveness. He added that my creation as cardinal had prompted him to write to me to tell me this.

I thought that that was beautiful. As you see, time does not belong to us.

Your Eminence, during your ministry to date, have you been able to assist women who have gone through the tragedy of abortion and to be a witness of mercy?

When talking to those who are involved in the good fight of promoting life, I often insist on the fact that we must always be very sensitive and attentive to persons who have in some way participated in an abortion. Indeed, many have committed this crime under the pressure of great anxiety. Certainly, we must insist on the seriousness of the sin, but with love for each person we must reassure the woman or the man who was involved in that terrible incident and tell them that God is merciful. Nothing here on earth is too far away for God. In my ministry as a confessor, I have often observed that a woman involved in an abortion has difficulty accepting God's forgiveness. When a woman understands the seriousness of the act that she has performed, an act that profoundly contradicts her essentially maternal nature, then she does indeed have difficulty forgiving herself and accepting God's forgiveness. Several women told me that at night they would hear the cries of their unborn child. We must understand and listen to the great suffering of women who have experienced an abortion and stand beside them as witnesses of divine mercy, of the unfathomable love of Jesus, who opens the riches of His Heart to those who, despite their sin, dare to turn to Him with trust.

Pope John Paul II compared abortion to the genocide of the Second World War. Some have taken offense at this perspective. We know that at the root of these evils there is the same refusal to respect human life from its conception until natural death. Can we extend this reflection by the Pope to euthanasia and, more broadly, to the culture of death that brings us closer to the totalitarian Communist and Nazi regimes?

Yes, there is a sort of totalitarianism connected with extreme individualism and the narcissistic isolation that destroys community. Everybody can become an annoyance to someone else. We are in danger then. I ask myself sometimes, because I am already of a certain age, what they will do with me when I am very frail. Truly, society is becoming violent and hostile. In its view, only the strong are free.

From the European and particularly the French perspective, Catholics in the United States have the reputation of being very uncompromising in their defense of human life and the family. France is the country of the so-called rights of man, which were promoted while they were massacring those who wanted to remain faithful to Christ; why is it difficult for France to understand the prophetic battle being waged by many lay faithful, priests, and bishops in the United States?

As an American, I received a lot from European culture, because during my youth the civilization and heritage of most Americans came from Europe and consequently from Christianity. Even today, in the middle of a time of secularization in society, America is still Christian. The Christian heritage remains. At the same time, the fundamental inspiration that shaped the Declaration of Independence of the United States included the idea that every human being has the right to life. Even today, Americans have this strong sense of the nature and divine origin of the human being. Despite all this, the fundamental principle is very much under attack today. France must react boldly and answer the question posed by Pope John Paul II: "France, eldest daughter of the Church, are you faithful to the promises of your baptism? Allow me to ask you: France, eldest daughter of the Church and instructor of peoples, are you faithful to the covenant with eternal wisdom for the benefit of mankind?"

Your Eminence, what would you say to those who are overly cautious, who hesitate to become involved openly in the pro-life cause and instead remain on the sidelines?

You must go back to the roots of the great history of Europe, which is fundamentally a Christian history, built on the conviction of the dignity of each human being. You must also have the courage to witness publicly to fundamental and essential things: the famous non-negotiable points listed by Pope Benedict XVI.

Can you restate these famous non-negotiable points?

The first point is to protect human life at all its stages, from the first moment of conception to natural death. The second point follows in recognizing and promoting the natural structure of the family—as a union between a man and a woman, founded on marriage—and defending it against attempts to make it legally equivalent to other radically different forms of union. In reality, other forms of union do harm to marriage and contribute to the destabilization of it by obscuring its specific character and irreplaceable social role. The final point is to protect the right of parents to educate their children.

On the subject of defending the family, I have a lot of admiration for the major movement in France, *La Manif pour tous* [The Protest for Everyone]. I saw and heard that French people in the streets were proclaiming the idea that same-sex unions are against the moral law. I dare say that I thought it was an ingenious message expressed by the drawing, or logo you might say, depicting parents and their children. The banners and the tee-shirts thus conveyed a magnificent message! The natural law was made accessible in a visible way: every child has the right to have a dad and a mom.

There was indeed a lot of creativity in the slogans used to defend the family. You might say, too, that some French people who never publicly stand up for anything found that they could be united on behalf of a common message, far from any partisan spirit. The current government, which wants to bring down Christian France, ran up against the common sense of millions of persons. Your Eminence, I take this occasion to ask you what, in your opinion, the mission of the bishop is in this context. Should he concentrate on intellectual reflection, or should he be in the midst of his sheep like the Good Shepherd?

In my opinion, the bishop should be in the midst of the faithful, teaching, witnessing, and encouraging people. I think that Cardinal Philippe Barbarin, Bishop Marc Aillet, and some other bishops have already participated in this sort of popular rally. In the United States, many bishops boldly go out into the streets. Every year a large number of them come to the March for Life in Washington, D.C. This is very important for the faithful, because the battle is hard. We have been fighting for more than forty years in the United States. There have already been fifty million killed by abortion. Do people really comprehend the nature of this tragedy? If they did, the faithful would have reason to be discouraged. They need to see that their bishops are convinced of the importance of giving constant public witness to their commitment to the cause of life.

In France, young people like to follow their pastors . . .

Yes, the bishop must write pastoral letters and must teach and preach. He must also go and meet the demonstrators in the field. That provides very strong encouragement, and the young people are very moved by the presence of the bishop and cannot forget it. In difficult moments, the bishop must be in the midst of his people. As Pope Francis would say, he must smell like his sheep.

Could there be higher imperatives that would lead us to set aside the fight for life?

Never! There is nothing more fundamental than the right to life. We must always fight for the cause of human life. No other cause can replace it. In the United States, opponents frequently mention the problems connected with poor health, poverty, or immigration. They have told us to limit or stop our involvement in the pro-life cause. My response is always this: the basis of social justice is respect for life. If we do not protect human life well, how can we defend health or the poor?

Among pro-life witnesses, are there any figures who seem to you particularly representative?

Mother Teresa of Calcutta, foundress of the Missionaries of Charity, is a very great pro-life figure. I recall having read, as a young priest, a book-length interview with her. I found in her testimony a very solid basis for involvement in pro-life activities. Then there are Professor Jérôme Lejeune, Jean Vanier, and others. I have been acquainted with families living with disabled persons. Thanks to them, I have been able to understand better that the disabled, if they inspire generosity, bring a wealth of radiant affection to all around them. Of course, there are other figures. We have had some bishops in the United States who went to prison

for their commitment to the service of life. I am thinking of
Bishop Austin Vaughan, an Auxiliary Bishop of New York.
There was also a Jewish physician who converted, Doctor
Bernard Nathanson. This former abortionist became a great
pro-life witness. There is Norma McCorvey, the plaintiff
"Jane Roe" in the infamous Supreme Court decision in
favor of abortion, who today is a militant activist in the
pro-life movement. This witness must always be calm and
strong: it bears fruit.

*Are there any religious communities working to defend human life?
Is this in your opinion a genuine charism? It seems to me that there
are not many such congregations. In France we have the Little Sisters of Catholic Maternity Hospitals (Petites Sœurs des maternités
catholiques), and there is also a plan by Bishop Aillet to found an
affiliated community. Presently, a young woman from the Diocese
of Bayonne, France, is preparing to serve the pro-life cause in consecrated life.*

Our great apostle was the Archbishop of New York, Cardinal John O'Connor. He was an example. He founded the
Congregation of the Sisters of Life. This congregation has
had a very impressive growth. It is very active and works
effectively.

*What is the connection with the current issues related to marriage
and the family?*

I do not see how it is possible to talk about the family without talking about the defense of human life. It is fundamental. Contraception and abortion are two stages in the attack
on conjugal love. In contraception there is a fear of new life,

and this practice often leads to abortion. It is of fundamental importance to associate works on behalf of the family with pro-life works, because marriage is the source of new life. The Lord created man and woman to love each other and to marry, and they express their love more fully in conjugal union, which is by nature procreative. It is very important for spouses to be firmly rooted in the moral doctrine of the Church. It is very important for their married life and their family life.

In what terms should we frame the question of civil disobedience and conscientious objection?

There are situations in which the Christian must disobey when civil law commands an action contrary to the moral law. He cannot obey a fundamentally unjust law. For example, in the United States, there is currently a crisis among the personnel of Catholic hospitals and clinics who refuse to cooperate in abortions or to prescribe contraceptives. Until now, it was possible to refuse a morally evil practice for reasons of conscience. It seems now that the government is trying to confine the practice of the faith to what goes on inside the walls of church buildings. It wants citizens to obey unjust laws. To that, I reply: We cannot do it.

Is it necessary to abandon the strictly political arena and become involved in other ways? There would be a great risk of aggravating the harmful laws.

We must look for possible ways of taking positions that are not contrary to the moral law. A Christian cannot do otherwise. Nevertheless, he can advance by small steps. Pope

John Paul II, in the Encyclical *Evangelium vitae*, speaks about politicians who cannot ensure that the moral law completely inspires the civil laws but can promote laws that are more just. We must do that. To abandon politics altogether would be a catastrophe. We must do everything possible so that Christians will be involved in politics, so as not to leave the legislative system in the hands of those who want to go against the natural law that is inscribed in the heart of man by the sovereign will of God.

I think that Catholic politicians must continue their formation in Church doctrine and be strongly committed to the sacramental life so as not to drift away little by little. I can only encourage them to have in their daily routine a time reserved for silent prayer and to set aside time each year for a retreat. This is indeed a good way of keeping a cool head with regard to temptations, whatever they may be. Ambition, giving into the seduction of the world, and seeking popularity with certain groups are not good. The example of Saint Louis can help those who are involved in public service. Some people in the United States have criticized me, saying that we should try not to reform the laws, but to instruct individuals. The truth is that the law forms the citizen and sets a direction for society. We must always try to change a law that is bad, without forgetting to provide the wherewithal to form hearts and consciences to respect the true good of the human being.

PART FIVE

Loving and Protecting the Family

If the family is the basic cell of society, isn't love at the heart of the family? If you could define love, what would you say it is?

Love is the gift of myself to another, the sacrifice of myself for the good of the other, the unselfish gift that looks to the good of the other regardless of my personal interest. Automatically, we think that love consists in the attraction of a man to a woman, and vice versa. But in order to be true love, this attraction is called to become ever purer and more unselfish, open to the larger circle of society. Authentic love comes from the Sacred Heart of Jesus, Who teaches us true love, to the point of giving one's life for someone else.

Is family consecration to the Sacred Heart still of particular interest?

In the dioceses of which I was bishop, I promoted as much as possible the consecration of families and of individual persons to the Sacred Heart. Many carried out this consecration. The testimonies that have come to my knowledge enabled me to appreciate the extent to which the Sacred Heart reconciles families and restores faith to those who have fallen away from it. The presence of the image of the Sacred Heart in the home and the prayers that may be recited, in a group or simply alone, bring the peace of Christ. This is one of the most ancient and most important devotions of the Church. To consecrate oneself to the Sacred Heart means to commit oneself to modeling one's life on the life of Jesus. The Sacred Heart shows us that we are never alone.

We are sometimes very far from true love. So many obstacles prevent us from giving everything to Christ. How can we grow in love?

Family prayer, especially the rosary, which is the source of great graces for all, is a special way of making God's love grow and spread among us. It is also good to have spontaneous spiritual conversations. You can start with the saint whose feast day it is or with the Blessed Virgin Mary. The essential thing is that this conversation be a common, everyday occurrence in the family. That way everyone can make progress. Many people have told me it is rare for them to spend time with their family, especially these days. I think that mealtimes can be special moments for meeting one another. To me it seems very important to organize one's time so as to allow for a real family life. That is fundamental. An increase of communication can cause love to grow and will make it possible to know others better. We need to know each other better so as to love each other better and to walk together toward Christ.

How can anyone persevere in love?

They say that young people today are incapable of lifelong commitment. The challenge for families today is to teach, to educate children to be able to respond to their vocation in life. Fidelity is learned at a very early age. In a culture that teaches you that you can change your spouse whenever you want, abandon the priesthood or the consecrated life, the stakes are high. Indeed, it is a matter of learning to promise to live out one's vocation for a whole lifetime. It is clear that, in order to do that, it is necessary to use the appropriate means. Children need to experience their parents' love for them and for each other, an unlimited, unconditional love. Each of us is made to give himself in a love that is faithful and indissoluble. That is something very beautiful.

Do you mean that children are first of all sensitive to the example set by their parents, even before the words they say?

Absolutely. Little children have a formidable capacity for intuition. They understand immediately, without a word, the love that motivates their parents.

The number of marriages is in free fall; very few young people become engaged. The great majority think that in order for love to last, it is necessary to have tried living together before marriage. Is this not a solution to the difficulties in making a commitment?

Secular research shows that cohabitation before marriage is very often associated with the later failure of the marriage. Indeed, it is understandable that living as husband and wife without being married destroys the mutual trust of the man and the woman with regard to the promises of marriage. You may wonder what the exchange of consent means for a couple who in fact have already lived together without having exchanged the consent that is the foundation of the marital union. In the context of general cohabitation before marriage, it is also understandable why many couples have so little interest in celebrating the sacrament of Matrimony.

Pope Francis recalled the importance of engagement lived out chastely before marriage . . .

Here are the Pope's exact words:

> An engagement focuses the will to preserve together something that must never be bought or sold, betrayed or abandoned, as enticing as the offer might be. (Wednesday Audience, May 27, 2015)

What we need for our children who are young men and young women is a serious, in-depth catechesis on the questions pertaining to human sexuality and the conjugal act, to marriage and its fruits, the family. Also needed is a catechesis for adults on the teaching of the Church concerning marriage and the family. When I was an adolescent, it was taken for granted that the only appropriate place for sexual union was within marriage. There was a very strong sense then of the conjugal meaning of the human body. Today, sexuality is considered a source of personal satisfaction, without any reference to its intrinsic conjugal meaning. The catechesis of children and young people is to a great extent shaped by the way in which their parents live.

People are waiting longer and longer to get married. Are young people today less mature than their parents were? Is there some frailty that did not exist before? Where does it come from?

There is no doubt that young people today mature less quickly than those in previous generations, because as they are growing up they do not take on responsibilities in the different areas of family life or family work, for example, on the farm or in a small store, as their parents did. Many young people today grow up without having to work hard or to make sacrifices for their family. This results in frailty with regard to the promises of marriage, which did not exist in the past. What is necessary, even in families that have a life of ease, is to assign responsibilities within the family that are adapted to the children and the young people and, as they grow up, to ask them to work hard and to sacrifice for the good of those who are in need.

More and more young people see marriage as an obstacle to their individual freedom or their desire for a career. Children are seen as a burden that one takes on only if it is not an obstacle to the rest. Is this right?

If you think that material goods and material comfort are the highest goods in life, that these are the goods that make us free, then marriage will certainly appear to be an obstacle to freedom, and children in marriage a burden. However, you do not have to live long to discover that what makes us truly happy and gives us freedom is pure, unselfish love of others, even at the cost of our comfort and our advantages. This is what the Pastoral Constitution on the Church in the Modern World meant when it declared that the procreation and the education of children are the crown of marital love. A young man or a young woman who grows up in a truly Christian family, and consequently matures in a love nourished by self-sacrifice, will immediately understand the beauty of giving one's life to another person in total love, in other words, a faithful, lifelong love, and in the context of that love welcoming new lives so as to educate them in a love similar to Christ's.

Should marriage preparation be strengthened? In your view, what are the essential points to insist on in this area?

In the context of contemporary culture, which is so secularized, materialistic, and exaggeratedly individualistic, given the often vacuous and imprecise catechesis that has been offered for more than fifty years, an extended preparation is necessary in order to get married. A couple preparing for marriage today needs an in-depth catechesis on the truth about marriage and on the demands that it makes on each of the spouses. In particular, it will be essential to insist on the importance of prayer and worship, on communion with God, so that His grace can inspire and strengthen the spouses and they may live in fidelity and forever remain in friendship with Him. We must recall the story of creation, when God created man and woman in His image to participate in His Trinitarian love.

In the present context, aren't many marriages actually null from the start?

It is difficult to say how many marriages are null from the moment when consent is exchanged. Human nature teaches us what marriage is: the union of one man and one woman, for life, in mutual fidelity that is open to procreation. Even in a culture where divorce is widespread, young people still have the sense that marriage should be for life. There are many today who, because they suffered much from the divorce of their parents, have a great desire for a lasting marriage. As for requests for a declaration of nullity of marriage, each one must be examined to determine whether or not it is well founded. There is no justification for saying that a certain percentage of marriages are null. That would open the door to a mentality favoring divorce, which would dissolve some valid marriages because no one investigates whether there are grounds for the request for a declaration of nullity.

Is the number of requests for declarations of nullity really increasing? What are the main reasons for them? Are these requests justified?

In fact, the number of requests for declarations of nullity has decreased. The reason for this is not clear. One of the factors, no doubt, is that, in an entirely secularized, relativistic culture, the question of truth is not taken into consideration. Be that as it may, a request for a declaration of nullity must have some ground to justify it, for example, the fact that one or the other party excluded from matrimonial consent either fidelity or indissolubility or the procreation of children, or else that one or the other party was incapable of giving valid matrimonial consent because of a serious psychological anomaly.

Don't most people think that a marriage that was valid to begin with can be annulled?

It is a sure truth that no one can dissolve or declare null a marriage that is valid and consummated. Actually, the procedure for declaring nullity of marriage exists in order to establish whether or not it is true that the marriage never was validly contracted, either because an essential element was lacking in the consent or else because the consent itself was not valid. The result of this procedure is not an annulment, as people too often say, because the word "annulment" implies that it is possible to annul something that exists. The exact term that should be used is "a declaration of nullity of marriage", in other words, the declaration that legitimate proofs have established that the petition is well founded.

In that case, is it really necessary to marry in the Church all couples who request it? Can a pastor sometimes legitimately refuse the grace of the sacrament?

In the Church, there is a prenuptial investigation, in which the two parties are questioned about their ability to give valid matrimonial consent and about their intention when they give this consent.

To refuse the grace of the sacrament would amount to refusing the sacrament itself, because [for baptized persons] there are not two different types of marriage, natural marriage and sacramental marriage. Sacramental marriage elevates natural marriage to its perfection and confers on it the grace necessary to live out the sacrament, but it does not change its essence. The grace of sacramental marriage gives couples the supernatural strength necessary to live the truth of marriage as God created it from the beginning (cf. Gen 2:24; Mt 19:4–6).

Many Catholics by now have gone through divorces while remaining attached to the Church. Do you think that the relation between doctrine and pastoral care, between mercy and truth, can be formulated calmly, without falling into caricature or polemics?

Yes, in some debates a dialectic may have been introduced between mercy and truth, discipline and doctrine. This contrast proves to be artificial and false. In order for authentic mercy to exist, it must be founded on the truth. At the same time, we can never say that doctrine remains when the discipline contradicts it, for example, when someone says: "I insist on the indissolubility of marriage, but in certain cases, persons who have separated from their legitimate spouse and have remarried can go to Eucharistic Communion."

How is it possible that a person bound by a marriage that has failed could start living with someone else without committing adultery or fornication? It is impossible. And so, we must know the particular situations, be merciful with the individuals, but invite those who are in this situation to convert and to rectify these matters according to Christ's law. Mercy is aimed at conversion, and the latter is always a conversion to the truth. Finally, there is no contradiction between doctrine and discipline, since the first inspires the second.

I also see another aspect of this problem: the suffering of the children, of those who are the victims of the divorced couples. Pastors must do their utmost to help these youngsters in their faith. You cannot help these youngsters respond to their vocation by in fact relativizing the value of the sacramental marriage of their parents. The testimony of the fidelity of one spouse, or of both, despite their separation, often bears fruit in the next generation. In honoring the truth of the sacrament of Matrimony, not only do we give glory to God, the source of all good, but we comfort and console the young people who have had to suffer through the disputes of their parents. Many children of separated couples who experienced that at least one of the parents remained faithful to the grace of the sacrament of Matrimony set out themselves on the path of Christian marriage or of a vocation to the consecrated life. Their suffering is then transformed into joy, for the children, certainly, but also for the parents.

In your view, therefore, the teaching repeated by Saint John Paul II on the question of divorced-and-remarried Catholics should not be called into question?

It is impossible to say anything other than what Saint John Paul II said. The state of life of divorced-and-remarried Catholics is not consistent with the mystery of the union of Christ and the Church. There is disharmony. Here is what Pope John Paul II says in paragraph 84 of *Familiaris consortio*:

> However, the Church reaffirms her practice, which is based upon Sacred Scripture, of not admitting to Eucharistic Communion divorced persons who have remarried. They are unable to be admitted thereto from the fact that their state and condition of life objectively contradict that union of love between Christ and the Church which is signified and effected by the Eucharist. . . . Reconciliation in the sacrament of Penance which would open the way to the Eucharist, can only be granted to those who, repenting of having broken the sign of the Covenant and of fidelity to Christ, are sincerely ready to undertake a way of life that is no longer in contradiction to the indissolubility of marriage. This means, in practice, that when, for serious reasons, such as for example the chil-

dren's upbringing, a man and a woman cannot satisfy the
obligation to separate, they "take on themselves the duty
to live in complete continence, that is, by abstinence from
the acts proper to married couples."

*Could the Church change her doctrine on this subject? If a pope
wanted to, could he?*

No, it is impossible for the Church to change her teaching
in matters concerning the indissolubility of marriage. The
Church, the Bride of Christ, obeys His words in chapter 19
of the Gospel of Saint Matthew, which are very clear insofar
as they concern the nature of marriage. No one disputes the
fact that these are the words of Christ Himself, and after
the response of the Apostles, the import of these words for
those who are called to married life is quite clear. In His
teaching on marriage, Christ explains that He is presenting
the truth about marriage as it was from the beginning, as
God willed it since the creation of man and woman. In other
words, the indissolubility of marriage is a matter pertaining
to natural law, to the law that God has written on the heart
of every human being. The Holy Father, as the successor
of Saint Peter in his pastoral responsibility for the Universal
Church, is the first among Christians to be bound to obey
Christ's word. They sometimes say that the Holy Father has
the fullness of authority (*plenitudo potestatis*) and that consequently he can change the teaching. But the fullness of
authority is not absolute power (*potestas absoluta*). It is the
fullness of the authority to teach, to sanctify, and to govern
in obedience to Christ, the head and pastor of the flock in
every place and in every age; the Holy Father is His vicar
here on earth. I recall the words of Saint John Paul II, when

such great pressure was exerted on him to change Church teaching about the exclusion of women from the reception of Holy Orders. He responded that the Church could not change this teaching, because it was the expression of Christ's will; then he explained this teaching.

Formation before marriage proves to be essential, does it not?

The formation of the faithful is indeed an enormous challenge. Just as the public authorities organize awareness campaigns to prevent the risks of cancer or traffic accidents, it is important that strengthening marriage, and encouragement to overcome the trials through which it will go sooner or later, should be on the agenda in the pastoral care of engaged and married couples.

When persons who do not have a well-formed conscience have entered into marriage without much understanding of it, having received little instruction from either their family or their pastors, how is it possible to help them on their way?

We have to start with catechesis to help them to discover the truth about the family and about marriage. This will not necessarily be easy for some, but it is the only way to help them to understand better what marriage is. We need a lot of catechetical programs for adults and spouses. Some movements, like the one called Retrouvaille in the United States, help couples who are having difficulties. They organize weekends of reflection on married life with assistants [i.e., couples who make presentations] and a priest [spiritual director]. Many marriages are saved through these moments of reflection and spiritual discovery. The importance of prayer should be mentioned, too. Those who commit themselves to reestablishing their marriage on Christ, in order to overcome their differences, realize that it cannot be an individual commitment. It has to be made together. In the United States, we have the movement of Teams of Our Lady, founded by Father Henri Caffarel. Father Caffarel did magnificent work. When I was a young priest, I read his *Letters to Young Couples*. It is very beautiful.

The Spiritual Exercises of Saint Ignatius help people to make progress in discovering God's will for marriage.

The Spiritual Exercises of Saint Ignatius are very useful for an initial reflection on one's state of life and the examination of conscience that leads to a commitment. As a second step, I would recommend the spirituality of Saint Thérèse of Lisieux and that of her parents, [Saints] Louis and Zélie Martin.

The relics of that saintly married couple were present during the recent session of the Extraordinary Synod on the Family.

Yes, in the chapel . . .

Do you think that the time for devotion to the Martins has arrived? Especially on the part of families?

I think so. With the canonization of Louis and Zélie Martin, we understand better where the sanctity of their children came from, especially of Saint Thérèse of the Child Jesus. It came from their married love and their relationship with the Lord. For my part, I have a special devotion to them;

every morning I pray to them for my family. I have the joy of owning a little relic of them, part of a piece of clothing, which was offered to me by some Irish Carmelite nuns.

Let us return, if you will, to the difficulties in marriage. Investigations into the canonical issues related to processes of nullity in marriage are sometimes very long and may even last several years. Isn't there a danger that the spouses, especially those who are weak in their faith and want to face the truth, might eventually become weary of the process?

The experience of the Apostolic Signatura, which assists all the ecclesiastical tribunals throughout the world, offers a wealth of instruction. When a tribunal has personnel who are well prepared to conduct the process, generally it does not last too long. At the same time, the process is for the parties a positive event in their search for the truth about their marriage.

Since the accusation made by one or both parties must be verified, each element in the process unfolds as it has developed over the centuries. Every step plays its role in the search for the truth. The process in itself is not really complicated. It would be more accurate to say that it is complex, because the situations are complex. When there is a very obvious situation, when it is a question of documentary proofs, then in that case the process is quicker. The essential thing is to have in every diocese serious, competent persons involved in running the tribunal correctly. That way they will truly be able to help wounded couples to know the truth about their marriage.

There are persons who have been married for a long time, thirty years or more, who ask for an declaration of nullity even though they have children or grandchildren. Does this not pose a problem?

It is difficult to understand how a declaration of nullity would be made after so many years of marriage, when there are descendants. It must be very difficult to prove. It is nevertheless possible, in the abstract, for some people to remain for long years in a marriage that could be declared null. At the same time, we must think about the possibility of scandal to the children, who in their family experienced the love of their parents, and of all the people who knew this couple and saw, experienced a true marital love. It is very difficult to accept that. Of course, it is necessary to say that the children born of such a marriage in good faith are legitimate, even though their parents' marriage is declared null. This happens sometimes in couples whose marriage has lasted twenty or thirty years, when the husband meets a young woman who takes an interest in him. That can turn his head. It is a human tragedy, in which it is not a matter of nullity but of sin, infidelity.

Many of our contemporaries find it difficult to refer to the example of parents who love each other, and this difficulty does not make commitment to marriage or consecrated life any easier; it hinders commitment. Today, nevertheless, we see many young families that have overcome the weaknesses encountered in their families of origin and have become staunch Catholics. In other words, do you think that this problem of Christian homes where there is disunity is at the root of the vocations crisis, too?

A young person called to religious or priestly life receives his vocation in the family, within the setting of the faithful, lasting love of his parents. A child who has experienced such a love in his family will not be afraid to respond to a vocation to the consecrated life. Nowadays, young people are widely acquainted with divorce and often experience the infidelity of their parents. They often are afraid now to commit themselves and afraid to be unfaithful in turn. When family life is strong and persevering, there are certainly many vocations.

You are acquainted with gender theory, the foundation of which is the denial of biological reality and the idea that "male" or "female" gender depends on the culture or else on a relationship of power, and not on any biological or anatomical reality. This ideology arrived here in Europe in particular from the United States, under the guidance of Judith Butler. Some French university professors, such as Fabienne Brugère, have been taken in, and Judith Butler has found consenting partners in France even in the Church. Some even think that they can reconcile it with Christian anthropology.

Gender theory is an invention, an artificial creation. It is impossible to have an identity that does not respect the proper nature of man and that of woman. It is madness that will cause immense damage in society and in the lives of those who support this theory. With gender theory, it is impossible to live in society. Already today, in certain places in the United States, anyone at all can change identity and say, "Today I am a man; tomorrow I will be a woman." That is truly madness. Some men insist on going into the women's rest rooms. That is inhuman. In the schools, you can imagine the confusion. A cardinal told me recently that one of his grandnephews, ten years old, on returning home after school, announced to his parents that he wanted to be a woman. He had quite simply heard talk about this theory in school and had taken it literally.

The homosexual lobbies are very much behind the promotion of gender theory. Do you think that it is possible to speak about homosexual love?

It must be said forcefully that so-called homosexual persons are in the first place persons. As such, they are capable of generosity, sensitivity, tenderness. Nonetheless, never has the word "love" been used so much in ways that distort it. It is clear that just because the word "love" appears in a sentence does not mean that it is truly a question of love. All that being said, it is impossible to speak of homosexual love per se. One can have friendship for persons of the same sex, but it is important to say that the love of friendship is not necessarily conjugal love. In the strict sense of the term, conjugal love is the summit of the love of friendship. When we speak of homosexual love as though it were a form of conjugal love, it is impossible because two men or two women cannot fulfill the characteristics of conjugal union.

What advice could be given to families who are affected by homosexuality in their children?

First of all, we have to show love and understanding, while at the same time saying very clearly that homosexual acts are serious sins, and consequently they cause serious harm to the human person. What causes homosexuality is a question that is both disputed and complex. Every person "must be accepted with respect, compassion, and sensitivity", as the *Catechism of the Catholic Church* teaches us (no. 2358). Every person has his own story and has lived through experiences that have contributed to the way he sees himself. The *Catechism* introduces the idea of cause and effect when, in describing the reasons why a person is attracted by persons of his sex, it speaks about the "psychological genesis" of the homosexual condition (no. 2357). Setting aside the inclination to sin, which is an effect of original sin, the Church rightly leaves to human sciences the study of the origin of this attraction, for this is not something that falls under the province of divine revelation or the natural moral law. It is clear, nevertheless, that when the *Catechism* uses the expression "psychological genesis", it opens the door to the study of the homosexual condition as part of authentic pastoral care. A "psychological genesis" rules out, from the Church's perspective, any "ontological" explanation of homosexuality. In other words, the Church does not agree that these persons are "born that way", to quote a popular expression.

In his *Letter to the Bishops of the Catholic Church on the Pastoral Care of Homosexual Persons*, Cardinal Joseph Ratzinger, Prefect of the Congregation for the Doctrine of the Faith, wrote:

> In a particular way, we would ask the bishops to support, with the means at their disposal, the development of appropriate forms of pastoral care for homosexual persons. These would include the assistance of the psychological, sociological and medical sciences, in full accord with the teaching of the Church. (§17)

It is necessary, therefore, to try to understand the causes for same-sex attraction: there may be difficulties in the relationship with the father, an overly possessive mother, a homosexual experience at an age when one is very impressionable, or sexual abuse. We must help young men and young women to understand better these attractions to their own sex, so that they might be convinced that they are not "born that way". The Lord did not create a "homosexual person", and therefore that cannot be someone's deepest identity. Such an attraction or inclination, although not a sin in itself, can only be understood as a wounding of nature that, if someone consents to it, leads to "intrinsically disordered acts", to repeat the words of the *Catechism* (no. 2357).

The teaching of the Church is not at all a moral condemnation or a judgment of the person who experiences this attraction or inclination. It simply means that in the case of an attraction toward a person of one's own sex, it is never licit to perform an act for the purpose of satisfying that attraction, because the design of nature applies to all human persons. Part of this design is the complementarity of the sexes and the sexual faculty's potential for procreation. Homosexual acts contradict this design, causing harm to those who engage in them and, in the final analysis, causing them suffering.

We do not want persons to remain enigmas to themselves, and this is why it is very useful for someone who experiences a homosexual attraction to arrive at a certain understanding of his inclination. The worst thing would be to accept this disordered attraction by being content to say to a person: "God created you that way, and therefore we must accept you as you are." Certainly, we must accept and love this person as a brother or a sister in Christ; but we must also acknowledge that he or she has been wounded at a crucial moment of life and that if the person follows his or her inclinations against the natural law, he or she will inevitably suffer as a result.

Today, a person who suffers from a homosexual condition must struggle to discover what authentic love means, especially in our era when the world is promoting the gender ideology. Nowadays there is enormous confusion, which is based on the false idea that there are practically an infinite number of possible sexual orientations. The twofold expression of the human person is not heterosexuality and homosexuality, but male and female. This is the authentic theology of anthropology: that God created man: "male and female he created them."

Finally, we must calm the parents: seeking to understand the origins of a homosexual attraction is not aimed at saddling someone with the responsibility for it or finding people to blame. The purpose is the truth, as well as the moral and spiritual healing that one finds when one humbly and courageously embraces that truth. It does not mean that it will always be possible to overcome that homosexual attraction; far from it. But it does offer a real hope of coming to understand oneself truly as well as a positive way that will allow their son or daughter to live out the Gospel in peace, in other words, in chastity.

You have often spoken also about a feminization of society. In the current confusion, are men adopting feminine stances, and women masculine attitudes?

Radical feminism denies that men and women have distinct gifts. It has been very powerful for several decades now, and in certain places, at least, it is accepted unreservedly. The result is that the distinctive gifts of a man have been eclipsed.

This leads to what is sometimes called "the fatherless society". The health of a society depends on an explicit identification of man as man and of woman as woman and on the recognition of the complementarity of their characteristics. The confusion of the distinct, complementary gifts of man and woman has especially devastating effects on family life.

Again, as part of this concern about formation, how do you envisage the continuity between the family, the school, and the parish? For the sake of coherence, what can be done to ensure that there is an unbroken thread connecting these three essential poles of family life?

There must be an obvious continuity that is as perfect as possible between education in the family and education in the school. The quality of the communication between the parents and the teachers must be manifested in visible cooperation, and the children will notice it right away. Everyone —the family, the school, the pastor, and the faithful involved in the life of the parish—must have a uniform approach to life, which springs from the unity of the faith. When there is a rupture between the school and the family, it creates immense confusion in the minds of the youngsters. I am thinking of that educator whom I met one day in the United States who told me that the family was a backward structure, detached from the real world, and that it was therefore necessary for the school to replace the parents and substitute for them. This is a very harmful point of view, which gives rise to real disasters. Parents, even with their faults (and we all have them), are the best educators to form the personalities of young people, their spiritual life, and to transmit a culture to them.

This is because God entrusted to them the children that they received from Him, and their mission is sacred.

When there were demonstrations organized by La Manif pour tous *in France several months ago, it was said that it is better to have "two nice dads" than a father and a mother who quarrel.*

The mistake that people make is to cite the example of failings that may exist in some families. Certainly, there are families with an absent, alcoholic father. If I may say so, the exceptions, the aberrations do not define what the rule ought to be. In the recent synod, for example, the tendency was sometimes to dwell at length on all the problems of the family, at the risk of speaking only about that, giving me the impression that the family I knew as a child, that the families I met during the first years of my priesthood no longer exist. I can tell you that there are many magnificent families that function well! Let us not forget that the Lord gives grace to families and that nature is well made anyway. I often observe this tendency to highlight what does not work instead of seeing what is going well. It is similar with the priests. Some people reflexively start from the cases of priests who have unfortunately abused a youngster and then say that all priests may be criminals in this way. In America, at least, the most frequent cases of child abuse are in the family and in the public schools.

In France, many entirely private schools are being founded—a trend that is becoming more and more difficult to miss. A while ago, I think, you blessed the cornerstone of an important Catholic institution in the vicinity of Paris, which is entirely free from State supervision. How do you explain this phenomenon?

The same thing is happening in America. Parents who understand very well the importance and the true nature of education are inspired to make many sacrifices to create a truly united school by gathering families with convictions for the integral formation of their youngsters. They want as complete an education as possible, rooted in faith in God and in knowledge of His law that governs the world and us, too. This is an impressive thing. In these schools, the parents greatly insist on the need for a good catechism and good academic formation.

You mentioned earlier your childhood and how liturgical life had had an impact on your growth in the love of God. What advice would you give to families? Should they give priority to the importance of their own parish by going to the closest Mass, or should they prefer a place that will be more appropriate?

It is important to look for a place where the liturgy is celebrated with true dignity and where it is clear that the liturgy is Christ's action. For the children, attending a Mass where the priest unfortunately thinks that he is the protagonist will destroy their sense of the liturgy. When they grow up, they will no longer want to go to Mass. You have children, and you know very well that they are very intuitive. If they have the sense that the Mass is a theatrical sort of activity, insisting excessively on the social dimension, that will not nourish their souls. It is better to look for a church where the priest intends to celebrate according to what the Church demands, according to the spirit of the liturgy.

Concretely, how can parents introduce into everyday family life the
Christian rituals that set a rhythm for the hours of the day?

This is very important, and it starts at dawn. At mealtimes,
there is the prayer of blessing the family and the food and
grace after meals. Another very effective devotion is the en-
thronement of the Sacred Heart with a prayer corner. It
takes just an icon, a statue, a candle, to facilitate gatherings
of the family, which will then pray for the world and for
those who are suffering. There is also the rosary. At the start,
reciting a decade is important to train the little ones, even if
it is difficult for the parents. With repetition and practice,
the recitation of the rosary becomes more and more beautiful. Every night, when a youngster goes to bed, have him
make his examination of conscience, recite the Act of Con-
trition, and say a prayer asking God for protection during
the night, because the night is the symbol of death, with a
host of temptations. I remember learning the prayer to Saint
Joseph for a happy death, which I still recite, incidentally. It
is also important to teach the child to develop a vivid sense
of the presence and protection of his guardian angel. The
very simple prayer to the guardian angel was something very
important for me, as far back as I can remember.

Often we say that we do not have the time . . .

You have to find time reserved exclusively to the Lord in
prayer. I have heard priests say: "My work is my prayer."
Yes, it is good to sanctify our work, but I fear that I will
not have the strength to sanctify my work and my everyday
life without dedicating a definite time to God—maybe a
half hour, for others fifteen minutes. At the end of the day,

when the children are in bed, you can find the time to read Sacred Scripture or a book of meditations. I can experience silence in the presence of God, telling myself that I am in God's hands. This is very important, consecrating the day to the Lord, especially for spouses. It is good for prayer to be individual as well as communal.

PART SIX

To Unite All Things in Christ

Ultimately you are telling us that it is necessary to "restore all things in Christ", the beautiful motto of Saint Pius X, the centenary of whose death we celebrated in 2014.

He was a great pope . . .

What sort of inspiration is Saint Pius X for you, a hundred years after his death? Is he outmoded?

For me, he is a great reformer in continuity. He reformed many aspects of Church life so that she might be more faithful to Tradition. One of his first acts was a *Motu proprio* on Sacred Music. He also had the insight that as soon as a child can recognize the Body of Christ in the Sacred Host, he is capable of making his First Holy Communion, which led him to revise the discipline on that precise point. He reformed canon law with great ingenuity, not to mention the Roman Curia, which he made more efficient. Even today we refer to *Sapienti consilio*. Furthermore, he was a great catechist. He reformed catechesis and wrote what we now call the *Catechism of Saint Pius X*. On Sundays, he used to teach the people of God in the Cortile San Damaso [a courtyard of the Apostolic Palace]. The people came from great distances to hear him. He wrote extensively on Sacred Scripture to promote Bible reading. He also confronted heresies, the aberrations of Modernism. Today, theologians say that he was not a great theologian. But when I read his documents on Modernism, I see that he understood many things, because a great number of errors that he identified are still current. To sum up, we could say that he was a fine example of a pastor of souls, *pastor animarum*. When we read his writings, his recommendations, everything is oriented toward the care of souls.

What can be done to help the lay faithful become truly aware of their mission, not to mention their specific vocation, namely, the Christian renewal of the temporal order, which is "to infuse a Christian spirit into the mentality, customs, laws and structures of the community in which one lives" (Vatican II, Decree on the Apostolate of the Laity, no. 13)?

The most important thing, for the laity, is to take above all else the Sacred Liturgy, prayer, and devotion as the source of their apostolate. From our contact with Christ through the liturgy, through prayer, through devotions, we receive the inspiration and the strength to bring Christ to others, first of all, in the family that is our immediate community. Christian life is by nature missionary. When you know the great joy that results from a relationship with Christ, it is impossible not to want to share it with others. I am thinking, for example, of Saint Thérèse of Lisieux. In the midst of her cloistered life, she maintained an immensely missionary soul. She thought of India, of the missionaries who proclaim the Gospel to the farthest ends of the world. We, too, must have this instinct: for us, mission territory is here, in a world that is no longer really Christian today. The world has changed, and we must re-Christianize ordinary everyday life, the economy, education, politics, and medicine. Priests cannot do everything. Priests must help the laity, and the lay people are the ones who will contribute to a great extent toward the transformation of the world.

This management of the temporal order . . . But how to explain the meaning of the social kingship of Jesus Christ, the doctrine that is the basis for the institution of the liturgical Solemnity of Christ the King?

Unfortunately, today the notion of kingship is disparaged. Yet it is a fundamental notion. In each one of us, there is something that reigns in our life, orients us, and is the most important thing for us. As our Lord said: "Where your treasure is, there will your heart be also" (Mt 6:21). The social kingship of Christ, my relationship and my friendship with Christ, gives meaning and direction to the other things in my life. We say that Christ reigns through His pierced Heart. His is a kingship of sacrificial love. There is also the notion of king that is quite contemporary. Indeed, Marxist rhetoric with its famous worldwide social justice no longer wants to hear anything about the king, who is associated with the oppression of the people. On the other hand, one of the saints with whom I am most familiar is Saint Louis, the king who invited the poor to his table to dine and who did much for the education of youth, not to mention Saint Stephen of Hungary or Saint Wenceslas.

Is it necessary for lay people to become active in politics? If they get involved, will they not lose their souls?

If we want to preserve the common good in society, it is extremely important that good, generous members of the lay faithful become active in politics. I recall how much Saint

John Paul II insisted in his Encyclical *Evangelium vitae* that it is essential for the family to become a more powerful political force so as to restore in society respect for the inviolable dignity of human life. Certainly, there is some danger in entering the field of politics, which unfortunately can be tainted with dishonesty and where the defense of certain selfish interests can win out over those of the common good. But we do not have the right to neglect our political responsibility because of the dangers. As the great political philosopher Edmund Burke said: "The only thing necessary for the triumph of evil is that good men do nothing." A layman can do much good for society if he relies on the help of God's grace, if he prays fervently to have the grace to be a good servant of his fellow citizens, and if he forms ties with other politicians who are true Christians. This will not be an easy task, because he will have to win the confidence of the people while insisting on what is just and good for society, even if a majority of his electorate seems to want something harmful, for example, abortion on demand or else the recognition of a same-sex union as marriage. Here, it seems to me, Christ's words in the Gospel are especially true: in carrying out the work of God's kingdom, we must be as innocent as doves and as wise as serpents.

Saint John Paul II urged families to be "the 'protagonists' of what is known as 'family politics' and assume responsibility for transforming society" (Apostolic Exhortation Familiaris consortio, *44). In your opinion, has this call been answered? Is it relevant today?*

This appeal by Pope John Paul II is prophetic and fundamental. I think that it has been answered in a sense, but not completely. This appeal should be repeated often in the

Church. It is necessary to insist upon it. Indeed, pastoral care of the family must be organized so as to emphasize the indispensable role of the family in the transformation of society. It is necessary to say again that life in the family is essential to the formation of youngsters. A propos, I can say that the formation that I received from my parents influenced me throughout my life. And so, in their families, through the love of the spouses, youngsters learn the way of sacrificial love, of peace in the community, as well as the virtues that you must have in order to occupy your place in society: honesty, modesty, willingness to make an effort.

Pope Francis often speaks about the Church's attention to the poor. How do you interpret what is called the preferential option for the poor—which presupposes a reflection on the nature of poverty.

Poverty is a material reality. When you have no means of feeding and clothing yourself, it is very difficult. But there is an even more serious kind of poverty, which is the lack of moral life: fornication and adultery, isolation, drugs, alcohol, prostitution, constant wandering in a life of vice, the emotional frailty of many young people who have sexual relations with multiple partners. Emotional instability is a terrible form of poverty.

Pope Francis put it well:

> No less a concern is *moral destitution*, which consists in slavery to vice and sin. How much pain is caused in families because one of their members—often a young person—is in thrall to alcohol, drugs, gambling or pornography! How many people no longer see meaning in life or prospects for the future, how many have lost hope! (Lenten Message 2014, dated December 26, 2013)

How can the priest, in his apostolate and his way of life, be a missionary of what Saint Francis of Assisi called Lady Poverty?

A priest who teaches the faith and morals of the Church humbly accepts a mystery greater than himself. He is self-effacing and makes himself very little, like a child who receives everything from his mother. His only wealth is his littleness, his poverty.

Pope Francis had some very strong words on the subject of the purity of intention and the detachment that priests and consecrated religious should have . . .

Here are the Pope's exact words:

> Woe to us if we seek consolation elsewhere! Woe to priests and religious, sisters and novices, consecrated men and women, when they seek consolation far from the Lord! . . . I want you to realize very clearly that if you look for consolation anywhere else, you will not be happy! (Address in Tirana, Albania, September 21, 2014)

The priest dispenses true riches by leading the people to whom he is sent toward prayer and the sacraments and helping those who are struggling in their moral life to stand up again. During the recent session of the Synod, some said: "We must go to the poorest of the poor to listen to them." Yes, of course, we must go out to meet the least ones, the suffering, but if we do not give them the truth, which is not "my" truth but rather the teaching of Christ, we will do only half of the job.

You spoke about the ethical relativism that affects our society. Might this not be the hour to address the question of the natural law? It seems to me that it received little consideration during the session of the Synod last autumn (i.e., in 2014).

The natural law is essential. You cannot speak about the family, marriage, the defense of life, without referring to it. Not to speak about the natural law is to deny reason. The Lord revealed His truth through reason and faith. There is no conflict between true reason and the faith. In order to grow in the faith and to understand the Lord's teaching, we must accept the purifications that our reason must go through. The notion of natural law is indispensable, and we must now restore this notion. Clearly, in a relativistic, materialistic world, people have lost the sense of nature, the sense that there is a law inscribed in things, which we must discover and follow. Pope Benedict XVI gave a fine speech in September 2011 to the Bundestag [parliament] in Berlin. He said, among other things: "Man does not create himself. He is intellect and will, but he is also nature." To speak about morality without having a sense of nature leads to a form of voluntarism.

No doubt you are also acquainted with the excellent book by Mary Eberstadt: *Adam and Eve after the Pill: Paradoxes of the Sexual Revolution*. Cardinal Timothy M. Dolan offered a copy to all the Fathers of the Extraordinary Synod on the Family.

Father Serge-Thomas Bonino, a Dominican friar, has written a very important document on this question of the natural law. In his study, he declares that the natural law "is not a closed and complete set of moral norms, but a source of constant guidance." He concludes his reflection in clear, accessible terms:

> The ultimate justification of the doctrine of natural law is found in a metaphysics that embraces the totality of what is real in the analogical unity of being which has its ultimate source in God.

This is very true. I am quite convinced that we must rediscover the meaning of the natural law. We are touching here on something very important. Maybe we ought to have highlighted it more during the recent [Extraordinary] Session of the Synod on the Family [in 2014]. In the same speech in Berlin, Pope Benedict XVI expresses his regret that so many refuse to consider the natural law:

> The idea of natural law is today viewed as a specifically Catholic doctrine, not worth bringing into the discussion in a non-Catholic environment, so that one feels almost ashamed even to mention the term.

More generally, do dioceses, parishes, seminaries devote enough time and assign enough importance to the social doctrine of the Church? Did Saint John Paul II not say that formation in the Church's social doctrine is a right and a duty for everyone? It is surprising, then, that this social doctrine of the Church has been neither diffused nor implemented as it ought to be in social, political, and cultural life.

Certainly, in the seminaries the students must learn the social doctrine of the Church. There is also the setting of the ongoing formation of priests, in which instructors should insist on the social teaching of the Church, which has its source in the kingship of Christ, in His plan to establish His kingdom in the world. We see also the unity of morality in respect for social justice. The *Compendium of the Social Doctrine of the Church* and *Caritas in veritate* are valuable tools. In the United States, in recent decades, there has been a development of moral theology separately from social justice. But the primary social justice is the protection of human life. What sense does it make to talk about health care, education, or other aspects concerning human dignity if human life itself is not protected?

Is there not a risk of confusing Christ's kingship with theocracy, as in Islam, which is unable to make a distinction between temporal and spiritual matters?

Christ shows us that His kingdom respects the rights of those who govern. Does He not say that we must give to Caesar the things that belong to Caesar? Our doctrine does not confuse the government of the State with religion. Religion respects those who govern but offers them the moral and theological principles that ought to guide them. In September 2010, during his pastoral visit in England, Pope Benedict XVI gave an excellent speech on the relation between State and religion and the necessity of a serious dialogue between the State and the spiritual authority for the good of society.

Your Eminence, about the Lord's response telling His Apostles to pay the tax due to Caesar: Caesar is subordinate to God. Christ extends His lordship over the entire universe, and Caesar must be subject to Him.

Caesar has his area of activity, but he must be guided by God and moral truth. I will answer you with two testimonies from the lives of the saints. There is, of course, the example of Saint Louis, who governed France as God's lieutenant on earth, and that of Saint Thomas More, who preferred to die beheaded than to betray the Gospel truth. Just before he was beheaded, he declared: "I die the King's good servant, and God's first." In other words, someone is a good servant of the king when he is first of all a good servant of God. There is no opposition between the service of God and the service of the king. In fact, one cannot serve the king without serving God at the same time.

Isn't the problem the confusion between the "sound laicism" of the State of which Pius XII spoke, and the laicism that increasingly imbues the surrounding culture and contaminates the political class, to the point where it becomes more and more difficult for a Catholic to refer, even implicitly, to the fundamental principles that are also the principles of the Church's social doctrine? Can the word "laicism" still be used today, inasmuch as it is very often synonymous with secularism and, therefore, with relativism?

The correct interpretation of the term laicism must be understood along the lines of the apostolate of lay persons in the world. The word "laicism" is derived from "layman". Indeed, the temporal domain, the apostolate in the world, is entrusted first of all to the laity. It is an apostolate that requires excellence in its various fields of activity. At the same time, this apostolate must be informed and animated by faith in God and love for His law. This laicism is of course just and necessary. There is another form of laicism, in which the laity understand their importance in the various fields of human activity but become proud. They think that God does not exist and that they can act without Him, apart from any reference to the divine law. The temptation then would be to live out one's faith, on the one hand, and to be active in society, on the other. The laity must have the humility to acknowledge the limits of their activity and, at the same time, to act as though everything depended on God's truth.

The economic crisis is an occasion for knowing better the value of earthly goods. Do you think that sharing wealth is a satisfactory response?

Sharing is a characteristic of the Church. The Church created the first hospitals and countless social works. The best form of aid to the poor is to support the works of the Church, for they are sustained by the love of Christ. I am thinking, for example, of the works of the Knights of Malta. Directed toward the sick and the poor, this work derives its strength from the charity of Christ. The United States has many Catholic institutions, hospitals, and universities. Today the government wants to impose norms that are against the moral law. In other words, it wants to destroy the Christian identity of these institutions. Nevertheless, those who have the means with which to help the poor must find a way of doing it so that their generosity is as effective as possible. The principle of subsidiarity proves indispensable in this regard: charity in the Church is managed, not in a bureaucratic fashion, but in a relation of proximity. Now, in the United States, mentalities are changing. People no longer really believe that the State will provide. This system does not work, because it is not animated by charity.

Is the autonomy of the lay person limitless? At election time, to what point can the faithful be bound by statements of their bishops?

It is necessary to distinguish between the true Magisterium and what groups of bishops say about certain practical aspects that are not objects of faith. One must always respect the bishops as such and what they say. In certain concrete matters, people are free to think in different ways. Lay people are free to exercise their practical judgment, according to a conscience that has been correctly formed by Catholic doctrine. An episcopal statement is not always invested with the authority of the moral doctrine of the Church. Pope Benedict XVI explained this well in his speech in Westminster, England, when he spoke about the relation between the State and religion. He said that the Church does not claim to meddle excessively in the affairs of the State, yet she must inform citizens about non-negotiable points.

Now you have left your post in the Roman Curia. Can a bishop or a cardinal be retired?

No, a bishop or a cardinal can never retire from his responsibility as pastor of the flock and, in particular, as a teacher of the faith. The circumstances in which he carries out his God-given vocation may change, but the responsibilities that result from the grace he has received never change. A bishop or a cardinal retires when our Lord calls him back to Himself through death. At that moment, he hopes to be able to say with Saint Paul: "I have fought the good fight, I have finished the race, I have kept the faith."

Your Eminence, what is your hope for the Church?

My hope is that the Church may be more and more faithful to her identity as the Bride of Christ in her teaching, in her worship, in her prayer and devotion, and in her moral life. My hope is that every branch of the vine, that every member of the Body of Christ, may become closer and closer to Christ and may know, love, and serve him, so that the glory of Christ may illumine our world, as we await His final coming, when he will return all creation to the Father, thus inaugurating "new heavens and a new earth".

p. 34 proportionalism & consequentialism